# Social Studies

The HighScope Preschool Curriculum

# Social Studies

*Ann S. Epstein, PhD*

HIGHSCOPE
PRESS ®

Ypsilanti, Michigan

Published by
**HighScope® Press**

A division of the
HighScope Educational Research Foundation
600 North River Street
Ypsilanti, Michigan 48198-2898
734.485.2000, FAX 734.485.0704

Orders: 800.40.PRESS; Fax: 800.442.4FAX; www.highscope.org
E-mail: *press@highscope.org*

*Editor:* Jennifer Burd
*Cover design, text design:* Judy Seling, Seling Design LLC
*Production:* Judy Seling, Seling Design; Kazuko Sacks, Profit Makers LLC
*Photography:*
Bob Foran — front cover, 1, 3, 5, 11, 18 (top right and bottom), 19 (bottom left), 21, 27, 29 (top), 33, 34, 35, 44, 47, 64, 67, 69
Gregory Fox — back cover (right), 7, 13, 18 (top left), 22, 24, 25, 29 (bottom), 40, 43, 50, 53, 55, 57, 60, 63, 65, 78, 80, 84
Pat Thompson — 45
HighScope Staff — All other photos

**Library of Congress Cataloging-in-Publication Data**
Epstein, Ann S.
  Social studies / Ann S. Epstein, PhD.
      pages cm. --  (The HighScope preschool curriculum)
  Includes bibliographical references.
  ISBN 978-1-57379-658-3 (soft cover : alk. paper)  1.  Social sciences--Study and teaching (Preschool) 2. Social sciences--Curricula.  I. Title.
  LB1140.5.S6E57 2012
  372.83044--dc23
                                            2012008212

Printed in the United States of America
10 9 8 7 6 5 4 3 2 1

# Contents

# Acknowledgments

Many people contributed their knowledge and skills to the publication of *Social Studies*. I want to thank the early childhood and other staff members who collaborated on creating the key developmental indicators (KDIs) in this content area: Beth Marshall, Sue Gainsley, Shannon Lockhart, Polly Neill, Kay Rush, Julie Hoelscher, and Emily Thompson. Among this group of colleagues, those who devoted special attention to reviewing the manuscript for this book were Polly Neill and Julie Hoelscher. Mary Hohmann, whose expertise informs many other HighScope curriculum books, also provided detailed feedback.

The developmental scaffolding charts in this volume — describing what children might do and say and how adults can support and gently extend their learning at different developmental levels — are invaluable contributions to the curriculum. I am grateful to Beth Marshall and Sue Gainsley for the extraordinary working relationship we forged in creating these charts. By bringing our unique experiences to this challenging process, we integrated knowledge about child development and effective classroom practices from the perspectives of research, teaching, training, and policy.

Thanks are also due to Nancy Brickman, who directed the editing and production of the book. I extend particular appreciation to Jennifer Burd, who edited the volume, and to Katie Bruckner, who assisted with all aspects of the publication process. I also want to acknowledge the following individuals for contributing to the book's visual appeal and reader friendliness: photographers Bob Foran and Gregory Fox, and graphic artists Judy Seling (book designer) and Kazuko Sacks (book production).

Finally, I extend sincerest thanks to all the teachers, trainers, children, and families whose participation in HighScope and other early childhood programs has contributed to the creation and authenticity of the HighScope Preschool Curriculum over the decades. I hope this book continues to support their social studies learning for many years to come.

# The Importance of
# Social Studies

# What Is Social Studies?

Children study their social world from the moment of birth and are quite sophisticated about observing and interpreting group behavior by the time they enter preschool. The early childhood classroom is a perfect setting for them to acquire the basic knowledge, skills, and attitudes they need to live in a complex society. Preschoolers learn about the people in their families, neighborhoods, and school. They begin to understand that social and environmental issues can affect them. Through age-appropriate experiences, preschool children develop the foundation they need to become responsible and fulfilled adult citizens.

Children's knowledge of **social studies** builds on their interactions with the people and materials in the preschool setting. They learn about human diversity through interacting with adults and peers, trying on different roles during pretend play, reading books, exploring the arts, and going on field trips. When preschoolers participate in the community of the classroom, they take part in a scaled-down version of the decision-making process in society at large. Taking care of the indoor and outdoor learning environment is a rehearsal for their becoming stewards of the planet. "In the preschool and primary years, social studies offer a structure for content [with] multiple entry points and significant opportunities for investigation. For children, such content serves as a training ground for acquiring problem-solving skills as well as a laboratory for the development and elaboration of interpersonal coping skills and strategies" (Mindes, 2005, p. 16).

Early childhood educator and HighScope field consultant Tricia Kruse (2010) says, "Young children are concrete thinkers so social studies is about building on what is relevant to their lives. Their everyday experiences help them develop a

## Social Studies in Action

At work time in the house area, Josh washes dolls and says to his teacher Zora, "My mom and dad already got married. They love me and I love them."

At work time at the sand table, Rex pours sand down a large cardboard tube and announces that he is "pouring cement on the foundation." Jenna brings him a hard hat and says, "You have to wear this because it's a construction hat. Here, put on your hard hat."

At work time in the art area, Hope and Tamika draw maps of the classroom with markers. They each draw different areas and tell their teacher Kay, "We're going to find a mystery. First we're going to the block area and then over to the house area."

At greeting time, Yvonne says to her teacher Emily, "When I'm in kindergarten, you can put on the message board that I won't be coming back."

At snacktime, Michael says, "Someone forgot to turn off the light. That's wasting energy."

sense of themselves and their world, which will continue to expand as they age. When children see, feel, taste, touch, smell, and otherwise actively engage with something, they can relate the experience to their current understanding of themselves" (p. 12). Just as preschoolers are curious about the scientific principles that govern the natural and physical world, they are eager to learn the social principles that govern society.

## Belonging to a Social World

After their family, the classroom is the first society that young children belong to. Its citizens get together several days a week to interact with one another, share activities and conversation, and solve problems. Teachers stand at the

> "Children are born into social studies. From birth, they begin exploring their world. At each stage of early development — infant, toddler, preschool, and primary — children look around and try to make sense of their social and physical environments. They gradually learn more about their expanding community and eventually come to see themselves as citizens."
>
> — Mindes (2005, p. 12)

head of the "government," but everyone has an opportunity to participate in the decision-making that determines how the small and stable society operates.

Building on their experiences at home and school, preschoolers become more sophisticated about the larger social world. They "decode"

*Greeting time provides an opportunity for children to learn about the social world of their classroom.*

behavioral norms and are sensitive to how individuals in social networks collaborate and depend upon one another. Preschoolers observe with interest the diversity and diverse roles among people. As their ability to express ideas and think critically grows, they begin to participate in the decision-making process. By making concrete connections to their own experiences, they become aware of how their lives occur at a specific time and in a particular place. With adult support, they find satisfaction in helping to care for the environment.

When adults build on preschoolers' meaningful experiences, children learn that their actions have an effect on the people close to them and on the wider world too. Then children like Josh develop an understanding of human love, Rex and Jenna imitate the roles they see grownups perform, Hope and Tamika navigate the classroom to play an intriguing mystery game they've invented, Yvonne pictures herself at a future point in time, and Michael begins to learn a simple lesson about caring for the planet. (See "Social Studies in Action" on p. 2.)

## Goals of Social Studies Education

The standards of the National Council for the Social Studies (NCSS; 2010) says "the aim of social studies is the promotion of civic competence — the knowledge, intellectual processes, and democratic dispositions required of students to be active and engaged participants in public life" (p. 1). Civic competence in turn depends on knowing one's community, having an inquiring mind, collecting and analyzing data, collaborating, making decisions, and problem-solving. According to the NCSS, effective social studies education should be part of the curriculum from pre-K through grade 12. Although NCSS offers only general early childhood standards (rather than differentiating preschool from the early primary grades), their definition of social studies is certainly applicable to the kinds of social learning that occur in the preschool classroom.

For example, preschool programs actively work to promote tolerance for diversity and encourage collaborative decision-making. As young children interact with others and take part in the daily routine, they develop basic ideas about community, justice, and democracy. These learning goals are recognized in the set of National Association for the Education of Young Children (NAEYC) accreditation criteria for "understanding ourselves, our communities, and the world" (NAEYC, 2005, 2.63–2.75). The importance that we as a society attach to these subjects explains why social studies is now a distinct content area in the early childhood curriculum standards of most states (Gronlund, 2006).

## Social Studies in the Early Childhood Curriculum

Because it is a relatively new area, the content and teaching methods appropriate to early social studies learning are still evolving. However, educators agree that children's development in this area parallels other subjects. That is, social studies learning moves from the simple to the complex, shifts from a focus on oneself to taking the perspectives of others, and involves learning specific content — in this case, about history, geography, economics, ecology, and civics (Seefeldt, Castle, & Falconer, 2010). Two curriculum components, both with cognitive dimensions, are especially important in the preschool years: social knowledge and understanding and social skills.

- *Social knowledge and understanding* is defined as an awareness of social norms and customs. Children must also have the cognitive capacity or self-awareness to recognize when their own behavior is (or is not) like that of others, and the emotional self-control to change their actions if needed. Acquiring this knowledge in the early years is called "socialization" or becoming a member of the community at home and in school. To become a participating member of the group, children must give up some individuality for the greater good, growing from a "me" to "we" orientation. This social-cognitive shift forms the foundation of civic competence.

- *Social skills* are strategies for interacting with others. Cognitive development, especially in perspective-taking and empathy, facilitates their acquisition. Classification skills — such as understanding similarities and differences, and the concepts "all," "some," and "none" — also help preschoolers appreciate how they are "like" and "not like" others. This combination of social and cognitive abilities allows children to observe and respect differences in gender, ethnicity, language, ability, and ideas. While their attention to diversity is very concrete, these early attitudes shape later abstract ideas about tolerance, fairness, and democratic principles.

*Preschoolers are capable of noticing and appreciating the differences and similarities between themselves and others.*

# About This Book

In the HighScope Preschool Curriculum, the content of children's learning is organized into eight areas: A. Approaches to Learning; B. Social and Emotional Development; C. Physical Development and Health; D. Language, Literacy, and Communication; E. Mathematics; F. Creative Arts; G. Science and Technology; and H. Social Studies. Within each content area, HighScope identifies **key developmental indicators (KDIs)** that are the building blocks of young children's thinking and reasoning.

The term *key developmental indicators* encapsulates HighScope's approach to early education. The word *key* refers to the fact that these are the meaningful ideas children should learn and experience. The second part of the term — *developmental* — conveys the idea that learning is gradual and cumulative. Learning follows a sequence, generally moving from simple to more complex knowledge and skills. Finally, we chose the term *indicators* to emphasize that educators need evidence that children are developing the knowledge, skills, and understanding considered important for school and life readiness. To plan appropriately for students and to evaluate program effectiveness, we need observable indicators of our impact on children.

This book is designed to help you as you guide and support young children's learning in the Social Studies content area in the HighScope Curriculum. This chapter provided insights from research literature on how children approach

social studies and summarized basic principles of how children acquire knowledge and skills. Chapter 2 describes general teaching strategies for Social Studies and provides an overview of the KDIs for this content area.

Chapters 3–8, respectively, provide specific teaching strategies for each of the six KDIs in Social Studies:

**53. Diversity:** Children understand that people have diverse characteristics, interests, and abilities.

**54. Community roles:** Children recognize that people have different roles and functions in the community.

**55. Decision making:** Children participate in making classroom decisions.

**56. Geography:** Children recognize and interpret features and locations in their environment.

**57. History:** Children understand past, present, and future.

**58. Ecology:** Children understand the importance of taking care of their environment.

At the end of each of these chapters is a chart showing ideas for scaffolding learning for that KDI. The chart will help you recognize the specific abilities that are developing at earlier, middle, and later stages of development and gives corresponding teaching strategies that adults can use to support and gently extend children's learning at each stage.

# HighScope Preschool Curriculum Content
## Key Developmental Indicators

## A. Approaches to Learning

1. **Initiative:** Children demonstrate initiative as they explore their world.

2. **Planning:** Children make plans and follow through on their intentions.

3. **Engagement:** Children focus on activities that interest them.

4. **Problem solving:** Children solve problems encountered in play.

5. **Use of resources:** Children gather information and formulate ideas about their world.

6. **Reflection:** Children reflect on their experiences.

## B. Social and Emotional Development

7. **Self-identity:** Children have a positive self-identity.

8. **Sense of competence:** Children feel they are competent.

9. **Emotions:** Children recognize, label, and regulate their feelings.

10. **Empathy:** Children demonstrate empathy toward others.

11. **Community:** Children participate in the community of the classroom.

12. **Building relationships:** Children build relationships with other children and adults.

13. **Cooperative play:** Children engage in cooperative play.

14. **Moral development:** Children develop an internal sense of right and wrong.

15. **Conflict resolution:** Children resolve social conflicts.

## C. Physical Development and Health

16. **Gross-motor skills:** Children demonstrate strength, flexibility, balance, and timing in using their large muscles.

17. **Fine-motor skills:** Children demonstrate dexterity and hand-eye coordination in using their small muscles.

18. **Body awareness:** Children know about their bodies and how to navigate them in space.

19. **Personal care:** Children carry out personal care routines on their own.

20. **Healthy behavior:** Children engage in healthy practices.

## D. Language, Literacy, and Communication[1]

21. **Comprehension:** Children understand language.

22. **Speaking:** Children express themselves using language.

23. **Vocabulary:** Children understand and use a variety of words and phrases.

24. **Phonological awareness:** Children identify distinct sounds in spoken language.

25. **Alphabetic knowledge:** Children identify letter names and their sounds.

26. **Reading:** Children read for pleasure and information.

27. **Concepts about print:** Children demonstrate knowledge about environmental print.

28. **Book knowledge:** Children demonstrate knowledge about books.

29. **Writing:** Children write for many different purposes.

30. **English language learning:** (If applicable) Children use English and their home language(s) (including sign language).

---

[1]Language, Literacy, and Communication KDIs 21–29 may be used for the child's home language(s) as well as English. KDI 30 refers specifically to English language learning.

## E.  Mathematics

31. **Number words and symbols:** Children recognize and use number words and symbols.

32. **Counting:** Children count things.

33. **Part-whole relationships:** Children combine and separate quantities of objects.

34. **Shapes:** Children identify, name, and describe shapes.

35. **Spatial awareness:** Children recognize spatial relationships among people and objects.

36. **Measuring:** Children measure to describe, compare, and order things.

37. **Unit:** Children understand and use the concept of unit.

38. **Patterns:** Children identify, describe, copy, complete, and create patterns.

39. **Data analysis:** Children use information about quantity to draw conclusions, make decisions, and solve problems.

## F.  Creative Arts

40. **Art:** Children express and represent what they observe, think, imagine, and feel through two- and three-dimensional art.

41. **Music:** Children express and represent what they observe, think, imagine, and feel through music.

42. **Movement:** Children express and represent what they observe, think, imagine, and feel through movement.

43. **Pretend play:** Children express and represent what they observe, think, imagine, and feel through pretend play.

44. **Appreciating the arts:** Children appreciate the creative arts.

## G.  Science and Technology

45. **Observing:** Children observe the materials and processes in their environment.

46. **Classifying:** Children classify materials, actions, people, and events.

47. **Experimenting:** Children experiment to test their ideas.

48. **Predicting:** Children predict what they expect will happen.

49. **Drawing conclusions:** Children draw conclusions based on their experiences and observations.

50. **Communicating ideas:** Children communicate their ideas about the characteristics of things and how they work.

51. **Natural and physical world:** Children gather knowledge about the natural and physical world.

52. **Tools and technology:** Children explore and use tools and technology.

## H.  Social Studies

53. **Diversity:** Children understand that people have diverse characteristics, interests, and abilities.

54. **Community roles:** Children recognize that people have different roles and functions in the community.

55. **Decision making:** Children participate in making classroom decisions.

56. **Geography:** Children recognize and interpret features and locations in their environment.

57. **History:** Children understand past, present, and future.

58. **Ecology:** Children understand the importance of taking care of their environment.

# CHAPTER 2

# General Teaching Strategies for Social Studies

# General Teaching Strategies

The terms "social studies," "socialization," and "society" share the Latin word root *socius*, which means companion, partner, sharing, fellowship, or union (*American Heritage Dictionary of the English Language*, 2000). Therefore, general teaching strategies that promote people joining together also form the content of social studies learning. As with the related areas of social development, the goal of social studies is to help children grow beyond their internal and individual focus to become aware of the principles that govern the social world around them.

Many curriculum components discussed elsewhere in this book contribute to developing social studies knowledge and skills. For example, sharing a consistent daily routine creates a sense of community, language learning emphasizes communication (both listening and speaking), conflict resolution and spatial awareness both involve perspective-taking, and art appreciation enhances an awareness of cultural diversity and different approaches to representing the world. All of these experiences help to build the civic competence that is seen as the goal of social studies education.

To apply these daily classroom experiences specifically to social studies learning, teachers can use the general teaching strategies described below.

## Build on concrete experiences to help children construct general principles for social understanding and behavior

While preschoolers are primarily concrete, object-oriented thinkers who focus on the here and now, research shows they are better at applying their "here-and-now" knowledge to other times and places than previously thought (Seefeldt et al, 2010). We also know from other content areas like literacy and science that young children can begin to engage with ideas beyond their direct range of experience. For example, they understand books and stories about real people living in places they have never been, or imaginary creatures doing things they have never done. They have ideas about how their bodies work inside or how people get sick, although they have never seen blood vessels or germs. In these cases, children draw on their own experiences (for example, they know that their homes look or smell differently from those of grandparents or friends) to mentally picture other people, places, or events.

In the same way, preschoolers can draw on their experiences to understand that people in other times and places lead lives that are similar in some ways but different in others from their own. They know from concrete cues — such as clothing, facial features, furniture, plants, and transportation — whether they are dealing with the here and now or the there and then. Furthermore, children begin to generalize from a specific incident to a general principle. In pretending to play store, for example, they construct concepts about how people perform their jobs and exchange goods and services for money.

*During work time in the block area, Liam, Shana, and Tallie build a fast-food drive-thru. Liam stands in the "window" and "swipes" the others' cards on his machine. Then he gives them "food," which they pretend to eat, before driving up to the window to buy more.*

Preschoolers gradually move from the concrete and specific to the general and abstract through meaningful conversation and thoughtful reflection. Thus the strategies that encourage children to speak with others (KDI 22. Speaking) and to reflect on situations, actions, and outcomes (KDI 6. Reflection), also help raise their awareness of the principles that guide human relationships in social studies. For example, when you talk with children at greeting time or snacktime about their home lives, they are learning that families have different living arrangements, home languages, jobs, cultural celebrations, religious beliefs, evening and weekend routines, and food and music preferences. From the specific examples children share with one another, they assemble a growing inventory upon which they can build the idea of complex social structures.

Children do not necessarily create these social structures on their own, however. Adults need to offer support as children talk about their experiences and explore the social ideas that result from them. You can offer comments and questions as children discover the similarities and differences in each other and their community,

and the social dynamics that affect their interactions. Here are some strategies you can use:

**Listen to and support children as they recognize similarities and differences in personal and family characteristics and lifestyles.** Wait until children raise the topic, then wonder why people do certain common things or do them in different ways ("Your dad stays home with your little brother, and your mom goes to an office"; "Juan's daddy is a teacher and Malcolm's daddy paints houses — people have different jobs"; "Leona walks down the street to visit her grandma, and Sally flies in an airplane to see hers").

**Encourage children to consider why people help and cooperate with one another.** Focus on familiar situations and events to help children reflect on social norms for behavior

*Children use the sand timer as they learn about the value of taking turns.*

("What do you think would happen if there were no traffic lights?"; "Suppose you could just walk into a store and take whatever you wanted without paying for it"; "I wonder why people put their dogs on leashes before taking them out for a walk"). Talk with children about the importance of cooperation and working together for the benefit of everyone in the classroom. Include them in making classroom decisions:

*At outside time, Matthew says, "I'm getting the big sand timer to have by the swings so we all get turns."*

*At work time in the house area, Frieda (the teacher) says, "Uh-oh, it looks like someone better get the broom and dustpan to get all the rice off the floor before someone slips." Sonya says, "I'll get it!" and Flynn chimes in, "I wanna hold the dustpan." Together, the children clean up the spilled rice.*

*At message board, the teacher points to the second message, which shows several children running indoors. One has fallen and has a sad face. The following conversation takes place:*

*Teacher: "Why do you think this child is sad?"*
*Child: "Because he hurt himself!"*
*Teacher: "How do you think he got hurt?"*
*Child: "He fell while he was running."*
*Teacher: Hmm. Can you think of ways we can keep kids from getting hurt?"*

*The children then offer several suggestions, including the idea that children should stop running in the classroom. They all agree this is a good idea. At work time, two children make "stop signs" they can hold up when other children start to run across the room.*

**Focus on the causes and outcomes of social actions.** Encourage children to consider why people behave in certain ways and the effects of their actions on others. For example, you might say, "Why do you think the other animals didn't help the Little Red Hen?" or "Suppose your parents said your baby brother/sister could play with all your toys" or "What if teachers didn't have to help clean up?" You could also try serving yourself most of the fruit in the bowl before passing it to the next person and seeing how the children react.

## Help children recognize that their personal actions can have a positive effect on the world

For children to accept responsibility for their behavior, they must believe their actions have an effect on others and the environment. When young children share control of the classroom with adults, they learn that their choices and actions matter and can result in observable outcomes. This model of shared control helps preschoolers feel "empowered." Taking responsibility for themselves and others becomes personal and meaningful to them.

It is important to focus on the positive outcomes of children's behavior. Too often, when parents and teachers talk about "consequences," the underlying message is that unsocial actions can have negative outcomes or effects. If we want children to feel empowered, we need to acknowledge their capacity to bring about positive changes. The following strategies can help children become aware of and appreciate the positive effects of their decisions.

**Comment on children's actions and acknowledge how they have helped individuals or the group.** When children are sensitive to the needs and feelings of others, they experience the "power" of relieving someone's distress or making them feel valued or happy.

*At dropoff time, Carl cries when his father leaves for work. Marianne takes his hand and says, "You can play with me until your daddy comes to get you." She gets a book for them to look at together, and later includes Carl in her plan for work time. The teacher comments to Marianne, "Carl stopped crying when you held his hand. He smiled a lot when the two of you played together in the house area." "I made him get happy again," says Marianne.*

**Acknowledge when children solve social problems so they and others can return to playing.** When children help generate and agree on solutions to social problems, they learn they are capable of creating win-win situations. Not only do they get their own needs met, they are successful in meeting the needs of others.

*At work time at the sand table, Robbie and Angel argue over the dump truck. With their teacher's help, they agree to use the sand timer to take turns. Their teacher comments, "You solved the problem!" A little while later, as the teacher checks to make sure the solution is working, she finds Robbie pouring sand in the truck while Angel drives it, then switching roles when the timer runs out. "I'm the driver and he's the dumper," explains Angel. "Yeah, and then I'll be the driver and Angel will be the dumper," exclaims Robbie. "You found a way to use the dump truck together," says their teacher.*

**Acknowledge children's voluntary efforts in the classroom.** Children have the opportunity to engage in many responsible acts when they participate in the community of the classroom. By taking part in cleanup, they have the satisfaction of helping care for communal property. The same applies to recycling materials to help to keep the planet and its inhabitants clean and safe. When the class writes a group thank-you note to a visitor or field-trip host, they are taking responsibility to extend their appreciation beyond the classroom walls.

*At the end of cleanup time, the teacher comments, "You put away the blocks and puzzles so fast today that we can go outside for five extra minutes!" "Let's do it fast again tomorrow," says one of the children. The class decides to time themselves for the next several days to see if they can keep adding extra minutes to outside time.*

Preschoolers' learning and actions in other content areas can also enrich people's lives and

*Even as preschoolers, children learn the value of responding to each other's needs.*

*As these children learn about plant ecology, they learn about taking care of the environment.*

give children the satisfaction of making a difference. For example, children make a positive contribution when they listen to others' stories and tell their own (literacy); make art for family members and appreciate the art that others create (creative arts); or say they want to grow up to be doctors to help sick people get better (science). The social studies curriculum can thus be integrated with other areas, and you can build on children's wide-ranging interests to support their social studies learning.

## Key Developmental Indicators in Social Studies

HighScope has six key developmental indicators (KDIs) in Social Studies: 53. Diversity, 54. Community roles, 55. Decision making, 56. Geography, 57. History, and 58. Ecology.

Chapters 3–8 discuss the knowledge and skills young children acquire in each of these KDIs and the specific teaching strategies adults can use to support their development. At the

## Key Developmental Indicators in Social Studies

### H. Social Studies

**53. Diversity:** Children understand that people have diverse characteristics, interests, and abilities.

**Description:** Children see similarities and differences in personal attributes (including gender, culture, age, religion, family structure, ability levels, and appearance) as natural and positive. They are interested in how people are the same and/or different from themselves and their families.

**54. Community roles:** Children recognize that people have different roles and functions in the community.

**Description:** Children know about familiar roles in the communities they belong to (e.g., family, school, neighborhood). They understand that people depend upon one another. Children know that people need money to buy goods and services.

**55. Decision making:** Children participate in making classroom decisions.

**Description:** Children understand that everyone has the right to share ideas and be heard. They participate as leaders and followers. With adult guidance, they join in class discussions, help make decisions, and share ideas to resolve group problems.

**56. Geography:** Children recognize and interpret features and locations in their environment.

**Description:** Children identify familiar landmarks (e.g., home, school, park) and navigate simple routes between them. They match objects and events to their locations (e.g., scissors/art area; outside time/ playground) and represent physical features (e.g., buildings, roads, bridges) in their play. Children use simple maps to describe and locate things in their environment (e.g., classroom areas, playground features).

**57. History:** Children understand past, present, and future.

**Description:** Children talk about what happened in the past (e.g., "Yesterday, when I was a baby…") and what will occur in the future (e.g., "When I'm bigger, I'll go to my sister's school"). They describe a sequence of events (e.g., "First I painted a picture, and then I built a tower").

**58. Ecology:** Children understand the importance of taking care of their environment.

**Description:** Children share responsibility for taking care of their environment inside and outside the classroom (e.g., picking up litter, watering plants, sorting things into recycling bins). They understand that their actions affect the well-being of the environment.

end of each chapter is a "scaffolding chart" with examples of what children might say and do at early, middle, and later stages of development, and how adults can scaffold their learning through appropriate support and gentle extensions. These charts offer additional ideas on how you might carry out the strategies in the following chapters during play and other interactions with children.

# Social Studies in Action

KDI 53. Diversity

KDI 55. Decision making

KDI 54. Community roles

KDI 56. Geography

KDI 57. History

KDI 58. Ecology

CHAPTER 3

KDI 53. Diversity

## H. Social Studies

### 53. Diversity: Children understand that people have diverse characteristics, interests, and abilities.

**Description:** Children see similarities and differences in personal attributes (including gender, culture, age, religion, family structure, ability levels, and appearance) as natural and positive. They are interested in how people are the same and/or different from themselves and their families.

At snacktime, Tommie says, "My mom is having a girl. I am a brother. I have a baby sister at home." Lenore says, "I have a baby sister at home too. Her name is Cleo."

At small-group time, Jacey draws a picture of herself and says, "I have green eyes. Just can't change them into blue eyes. Latrelle and Jonah have brown eyes. They can't change them either." Jonah counters, "Uh, uh. When I grow up I'm gonna have blue eyes like my dad."

At greeting time, Sherelle announces, "When I grow up, I'm going to be a daddy so I can have tickly whiskers."

At work time in the house area, Sara demonstrates to Maria with play dough how to make potato pancakes. "First you chop up the potatoes and then you fry them up in a pan." Maria in turn shows Sara how to bake Christmas cookies. "Roll them flat and spread them out on here (a cookie sheet). Then you stick them in the oven until they smell."

From an early age, children are aware of similarities and differences in themselves and others — at home, in school, and in the community. Preschoolers recognize that diversity in such things as gender, culture, ethnicity, religion, and special needs are associated with differences in appearance, beliefs, and behavior. By this age they have already begun to internalize popular norms and stereotypes about which traits are considered more desirable and are aware of many common attributes that determine "in-group" and "out-group" membership (Aboud, 2003, 2005).

Children's emerging classification abilities can both help and hinder their openness to diversity. On the one hand, they are curious about what makes them and their families "like" and "not like" others. They enjoy discovering new characteristics and sorting people based on individual and group attributes. On the other hand, because their categories can be quite rigid, preschoolers may label things "good" and "bad" rather than merely different. "Listening to their ideas helps us pick up where they are confused and suggests how we can make their understanding more accurate. While working with children to expand and correct their ideas, it is also important to be respectful of the intelligence that underlies their attempts to make sense of what they experience" (Derman-Sparks & Edwards, 2010, p. 14). As early childhood educators, we want them to appreciate and accept diversity, not judge it. "Respecting diversity means treating people as individuals, not as stereotypes, and recognizing that individuals can simultaneously share some characteristics and differ on others" (Epstein, 2009, p. 91).

## Developing Ideas About Diversity

Young children's understanding of diversity reflects their general level of cognitive development and social understanding. They apply many of the same thought processes they bring to classifying objects and events to their ideas about people and their attributes (how others look, act, and think). The following thought patterns characterize children's emerging concepts about human diversity (Epstein, 2009; Levin, 2003):

- *Children begin to construct ideas about similarities and differences when they are very young.* Infants differentiate parents from strangers, they begin labeling gender at age two, and their ideas about ethnicity, religion, and special needs begin to emerge at age three.

- *Young children begin by focusing on one attribute at a time, usually an obvious visible one.* Children attend to obvious characteristics, especially visual ones, in classifying people. For example, they judge gender by clothing or hairstyle rather than by bodily features, and they judge special needs by whether people use assistive devices rather than physiological conditions.

- *Young children think in dichotomies.* Children see people as being either the same or different. Not until later in preschool, when children are able to classify on more than one dimension, can they accept that people can be the same in some ways but different in others.

- *Young children cannot always differentiate permanent from changeable characteristics.* Because they are still learning about the natural and physical world, children do not always know what makes an attribute fixed or flexible. Thus they may think that skin color can be washed away or that gender can change when people grow up. Conversely, children may believe families must eat certain foods or dress a particular way because of where they are from.

## Societal Influences on Children's Attitudes About Diversity

How children think about and respond to diversity is influenced by what they see and hear in the world around them. Although we often romanticize children's automatic acceptance of everyone, they internalize stereotypes and may adopt negative attitudes quite early (Banks, 1993). The sources of children's ideas about diversity are their families and, increasingly, the popular media (Carlsson-Paige, 2008). However, early childhood program experiences — and how these are mediated by adults — can also have a profound effect on the development of their attitudes toward themselves and others. Early beliefs tend to persist, which is why "early childhood educators have the best opportunity to positively influence the racial and ethnic attitudes of children" (Soto, 1999, p. 225).

*Young children develop their thinking about diversity using the same thought processes they bring to classifying objects and events.*

# Teaching Strategies That Support Diversity

The makeup of early childhood programs today is increasingly diverse. Children in the same classroom may represent different ethnic groups, countries of origin, languages, religions, and family composition. Educators need and want to help young children understand and appreciate the pluralistic society we live in. Beginning with the Anti-Bias Curriculum (Derman-Sparks, 1989), a growing number of publications explicitly address these concerns with organizational and classroom policies to broaden awareness and acceptance (Derman-Sparks & Edwards, 2010; Gonzalez-Mena, 2008). "Multicultural education emphasizes the positive, adaptive value of cultural pluralism....The underlying premise is that exposing children to a wide range of values and lifestyles will help them appreciate their own and other groups" (Ramsey, 2006, p. 280).

Despite a growing number of resources, however, many teachers are uncomfortable dealing with diversity issues in the classroom. They may assume children's attitudes originate at home or are so heavily influenced by the media that educators are powerless to change them. Or teachers may be tempted to lecture young children about the virtues of treating everyone with respect. The first approach accomplishes nothing and the second is ineffective. Instead, to forthrightly address human differences, teachers need to understand how young children construct ideas about others. Then they need to facilitate positive experiences so preschoolers will generalize from being open toward individuals to accepting categories of people as a whole. The following strategies allow teachers to help young children understand and appreciate diversity among people.

## Model respect for diversity

If we want children to treat others equally and fairly, the first step is to demonstrate this behavior ourselves. Teachers should listen to and accept the ideas and feelings of everyone, not only the children but also parents and colleagues. Gonzalez-Mena (2007) says teachers need to stop "operating out of unconscious systems" (p. 3) based on their own unexamined beliefs of what is "right." If adults instead suspend judgments and are open-minded about understanding different perspectives, they create a climate of respect that children can copy and then adopt as their own.

Disrespect for differences is often rooted in fear. Children, like adults, may be uncomfortable with people and practices that are unfamiliar, and a natural tendency is to label what feels strange as "bad." However, if adults make exploring differences part of everyday classroom interactions, young children will not automatically equate "different" with "bad." Rather, finding out about one another's appearance, behaviors, and beliefs will become just another area of learning.

**Creating an emotionally safe environment.** The backdrop for this learning must be emotionally safe. To create such an environment, model using neutral and factual words to describe differences ("Kulani has curly hair and Frank has straight hair"; "Jonathan's family eats ham on Christmas and Eli's family eats potato latkes on Hanukkah"; "Julia has two mommies, and Boris lives with his mother, father, and two aunts"). Solicit information rather than making assumptions about beliefs and practices ("Does your family celebrate birthdays? What do they like to do?"). Never criticize or imply that one look, idea, or practice is better than another. If children make hurtful comments ("Crystal has dirty skin"), reframe them as you would when resolving social conflicts (KDI 15. Conflict resolution) ("Crystal's skin is darker than yours and mine. Skin comes in many different colors"). Remember that young children do not intend harm when they make such statements. They are trying to understand the nature of people and, as with all social learning, they sometimes make mistakes.

*In an emotionally safe environment, children interact and explore their similarities and differences.*

**Challenging stereotypes.** Nevertheless, when children do express negative stereotypes, it is okay to gently challenge their reasoning (Levin, 2003). Pointing out contradictions helps them reexamine their thinking, just as this strategy can be used to scaffold early mathematics or science reasoning. Don't correct children or say they are wrong. Instead, you might comment that what they say or think seems to be at odds with another observation or experience. For example, if a child says "old people smell bad," you might ask around the table whether children's grandparents (or the gray-haired cook) smell bad. The responses, especially when they come from peers, can help a child reconsider the accuracy of his or her statement. At the same time, don't feel you have to "fix" children's biases and stereotypes or answer all their questions directly. Encourage children to explore ideas with one another and arrive at conclusions through their own experiences.

**Teddy:** *(To Rachel)* I get Christmas presents and you don't!

**Teacher:** *(To Teddy)* You are happy when your parents give you Christmas presents. *(To Rachel)* What makes you happy on Hanukkah?

**Rachel:** *(To teacher and Teddy)* When I win the dreidl game!

**Teddy:** *(To Rachel)* What's that?

**Rachel:** *(To Teddy)* You spin it and you win pennies!

**Teacher:** *(To both children)* I'll bring in a dreidl for us to play with tomorrow.

**Teddy:** *(To Rachel)* Will you show me how to play it?

**Ariana:** *(To Wendy, in a wheelchair)* I can run really fast on the grass and you can't.

**Teacher:** *(To Ariana)* It makes you feel good to run fast at outside time. *(To Wendy)* What do you like best about being outside?

**Wendy:** *(To teacher and Ariana)* I can go super-fast on the path in my wheelchair. The motor helps me go up the hill.

**Ariana:** *(To Wendy)* Can I try it? *(She puts her hand on the arm of the wheelchair.)*

**Wendy:** *(To Ariana)* I don't know. I have to ask my mom when she gets here.

**Teacher:** *(To both children)* I know where I can borrow a child-sized wheelchair for the class to use. But it doesn't have a motor like Wendy's, so we may have to help push each other.

**Wendy:** *(To Ariana)* Maybe I can push your wheelchair with my wheelchair!

Finally, just as we treat children with respect and want them to be respectful toward one another, children should observe us acting respectfully toward other adults. Our words and our acts should convey this respect, whether it is using a parent's preferred term of address ("Mrs. Smith" rather than "Mary") or providing program brochures in language(s) other than English. Be especially self-aware of judging or dismissing people based on status. When preschoolers see a supervisor being impatient with a teacher, or a teacher being curt with a parent, they learn that rudeness or disrespect is an acceptable or even a "grown-up" way to act. To model a respect for diversity, our body language as well as our words should be both consistent and inclusive.

## Focus on similarities and differences without judgmental comparisons

Since children are inherently curious about differences, you can use their observations as learning opportunities. Treat differences among people factually as you would variations among materials and events. Comment on specific attributes and accomplishments without labeling one as better than the other. For example, "Yolanda is wearing red ribbons, and Nicole's braids have blue ribbons" is a neutral statement. By contrast, if you say to Yolanda, "I like red ribbons," then Nicole may infer there is something wrong or inferior about her blue ones.

Remember that diversity is about similarities as well as differences — what people share as well as what distinguishes them. For example, everyone eats, but we prefer different foods. Eating utensils come in many shapes and forms; some people eat with their fingers. Since preschoolers are concrete thinkers, comment on characteristics they can see, hear, taste, touch, and smell. Connect your observations to their experiences by commenting, for example, on where and what children plan to do at work time, food preferences at snacktime, who lives in their households, or family meal and bedtime routines.

Ann Epstein (2009) gives an example in which a child named Abby tells her teacher Deirdre that she has a father "who doesn't live with us." She then tells Deirdre about her visits with him:

**Abby:** He picks me up here. His car is bigger than my mommy's.

**Deirdre:** I see his big car when he comes to get you. It's dark green.

**Abby:** He has a special seat for me in the back. And we go shopping on the way to his apartment.

**Deirdre:** What do you buy?

**Abby:** Spaghetti, every time spaghetti. And donuts. My mommy doesn't let me eat donuts.

**Deirdre:** Mommies and daddies sometimes have different rules.

**Abby:** My daddy also lets me watch one extra television show. But not too much. And he reads to me before I go to sleep, just like at home with my mommy" (p. 95).

*In the house area, include toys and other items that reflect diverse cultures and backgrounds.*

Draw on the diversity in the classroom to help children appreciate differences. Even if some traits are homogeneous (children are the same ethnicity or speak the same language), engage them in discussing other types of difference such as gender, color and food preferences, or family composition. For variations that are not present in your classroom but that children are likely to encounter elsewhere (people walking with canes or speaking other languages at the supermarket), find other meaningful and concrete ways to introduce them. Examples include picture books, photographs, artwork, computer programs, field trips, and visitors.

## Include diversity in every classroom area and activity

Many well-intentioned programs introduce "diversity" in connection with holidays or traditional foods or clothing. However, kimonos in the dress-up area, hummus at snacktime, or a parent talking about Kwanza, while valuable experiences, do not help children understand that diversity is an everyday and everywhere occurrence. Our goal as educators is to treat diversity as the norm, not the exception. Therefore, an effective approach to diversity is to represent it in the daily lives of people instead of focusing on a "tourist curriculum" approach (Gronlund, 2006).

Make sure that the equipment and materials in the learning environment reflect the children's homes and community. Families can often contribute many of these items. For example:

- In the house area, provide work clothes and tools used in various jobs, cooking utensils and empty food containers from many ethnic cuisines, and equipment used by people with disabilities (crutches, magnifying glasses for reading).

- At snacktime and meals, serve food from different cultures and religions on a regular basis, not just as special treats associated with holidays.

- In the reading area, feature books, magazines, and catalogs with realistic illustrations and photographs of diverse cultures, people performing nonstereotypical jobs, families of varying composition and backgrounds, and people of different ages. Make sure the images in computer programs also reflect this diversity.

- Encourage families to bring seeds for their favorite vegetables and flowers to plant in the school garden.

- Hang reproductions of artwork from around the world at eye level throughout the room. Include simple instruments from different traditions in the music area. Listen and move to music from different cultures and genres.

- Take field trips to stores and outdoor markets that serve the local population. Attend street fairs, art and craft shows, concerts, and festivals that celebrate the community's diversity. Celebrate holidays and traditions observed by families that are important and meaningful to the children.

For examples of how young children demonstrate their awareness and acceptance of diversity at different levels of development and how adults can scaffold preschoolers' diversity learning, see "Ideas for Scaffolding KDI 53. Diversity" on page 32. Use the suggestions in the chart to support and gently extend children's learning during your daily play and other interactions with them.

## When and How to Celebrate Holidays

Celebrating holidays can pose a dilemma in early childhood programs. Holidays are usually happy occasions and are a natural way to honor diversity. However, if they are also religious observances, publicly funded programs must adhere to laws regulating separation of church and state. Further, families that don't observe a particular holiday may feel excluded. There is also the issue that holidays that are a "big deal" for grown-ups may hold limited interest for young children. Or conversely, that holidays adults have long since crossed off their calendars continue to engage children's imaginations and dominate their role playing.

In the following vignette, two preschool teachers (the "we" in the narrative) not only resolved the problem of how to celebrate holidays but even expanded their definition of celebrations. Both adults and children learned something in the process.

### "Rosie Celebrates Christmas, Irene Celebrates Santa, and I Celebrate Hanukkah!"

*This comment, made by three-year-old Eli, illustrates the importance that holidays and other special celebrations can have for a young child. Like many preschoolers, Eli was already becoming aware that individuals and families have many different ways of observing these special events.*

*If being interested in celebrations is natural for young children, why do so many adults feel panicky when deciding whether or how to support holiday-related experiences in their early childhood setting?*

*We used to feel this concern every time a holiday was near. Until we thought through our approach to these special occasions, the word "celebration" left us feeling uneasy and unsure. We questioned ourselves: How did we decide what to celebrate? What experiences with holidays and special events had the children in our classroom participated in? Would we offend some families by celebrating holidays that have a religious basis? How would we support the child in our classroom who did not celebrate any holidays due to religion? And, if we did decide to bring such celebrations into our classroom, how could we use what we knew about active learning to enhance these experiences?*

*It would have been easy to "bury our heads in the sand" and have no holiday celebrations. Then again, we could have taken the "holiday of the month" approach and celebrated every holiday on the calendar. Instead we decided to find a middle ground: In the holiday-related experiences we planned, we tried to show the value we placed on the traditions, rituals, and beliefs of the children and families*

*in our classroom, without losing sight of the fact that these traditional celebrations raised sensitive issues for many families.*

*Here are some of the steps we took as we explored this issue:*

**Defining celebrations.** *Special occasions seemed to us to be divided into two categories: The first included the standard ways of observing holidays that had religious, cultural, or ethnic origins; the second we called "life's little celebrations." This second category included traditions and rituals that were less oriented to specific groups or days on the calendar — things like Kyle's family having a shower for a new baby, Jessie's grandmother teaching her how to make paper towel butterflies, and the arrival each summer of ripe red tomatoes in the preschool garden. We also remembered other kinds of special occasions — the arrival of new siblings, riding a "two-wheeler" for the first time, attending community art fairs and carnivals, and losing a tooth.*

*We then recalled how excited Lauren was about being a flower girl in her aunt's wedding. We celebrated with Lauren by sharing her excitement, listening to her stories of the wedding, and eventually adding veils and flowers to the house area for her to reenact the wedding. In a similar way, we celebrated with Lakisha when she made piles of*

**Using families as resources.** *Through home visits, family surveys, casual conversations with family members at dropoff and pickup times, parent-teacher conferences, and family potlucks and gatherings, we had already established an open relationship with our families. We resolved to use these ways to learn more about how they observed holidays and family traditions. For example, one day Katie's mother mentioned at dropoff time that Katie had made and taped paper Easter eggs to the walls in the living room. She also mentioned that their family would be dyeing Easter eggs and that she would be happy to bring eggs and help dye them with the class. We invited Katie's mom to dye eggs with the children at small-group time and added colored plastic eggs and baskets to the house area. In the days that followed, the children invented a "hide-the-egg" game.*

*Since we have adopted our new approach to holidays, the word "celebration" no longer evokes panic and uneasiness for us. We invite you to try this approach in your own early childhood center. As your starting point, know the families in your classroom, and keep your children's interests in mind. Most of all, understand — as Eli did — that we all celebrate in our own way and that's okay!*

— Adapted from Lucier & Gainsley
(2005, pp. 433–441)

*toys in the house area and said, "I'm packing for my trip to Grandma and Grandpa's house." Lakisha's family always took a trip to her grandparents' house for Thanksgiving weekend. To support Lakisha's family tradition, we added suitcases and a car steering wheel to the classroom.*

**Recognizing why celebrations are important.** *We discovered several reasons why celebrations are important. (1) Celebrations add excitement to everyday life. (2) They make children and families feel important and special. (3) They introduce children to new routines and rituals. (4) They pass on family cultures and traditions. (5) They expose children to differences among people. (6) They offer opportunities for people to recognize their similarities. (7) They help children connect with the communities in which they live.*

# Ideas for Scaffolding KDI 53. Diversity

Always support children at their current level and occasionally offer a gentle extension.

| Earlier | Middle | Later |
| --- | --- | --- |
| *Children may* | *Children may* | *Children may* |
| • Identify one observable personal characteristic in someone else (e.g., "Jason is a boy"; "Karl has black hair").<br><br>• Play what is familiar to their own family (e.g., make dog sounds if their family has a dog). | • Identify a personal characteristic people have in common (e.g., "Hey, you've got a sister and so does Cory!"; "We both have dark skin").<br><br>• Express interest in another person's family characteristics (e.g., "I ate round bread when I went to Sunil's house"; "What's your brother's name?"). | • Identify personal characteristics that differentiate people (i.e., traits that they do not have in common; e.g., "You have Christmas and I do Hanukkah").<br><br>• Compare their own and others' family characteristics (e.g., put their arms alongside each other to compare skin color; "I have a swing set in my yard. When I go to Lori's apartment, we go to the playground and have to share with other kids"). |
| *To support children's current level, adults can* | *To support children's current level, adults can* | *To support children's current level, adults can* |
| • Acknowledge children's observations about a characteristic of another person (e.g., "Yes, Jason is a boy").<br><br>• Provide pretend play materials that reflect the children's family cultures and traditions (e.g., uniforms for different types of jobs in the dress-up area; cooking utensils and empty food containers from different cuisines in the house area). | • Affirm children's observations about shared characteristics (e.g., "Yes, you're both boys"); use a personal characteristic during a transition (e.g., "Everyone who is going to kindergarten next year, go to the rug").<br><br>• Acquaint children with one another's families (e.g., invite children to bring in pictures of their families doing everyday and special things such as playing catch, cooking dinner, camping). | • Encourage children to identify characteristics people do not have in common (e.g., "Who in our small group does not have curly hair?").<br><br>• Talk about the variety of family characteristics in the class during conversations throughout the day (e.g., at snacktime, talk about what children's families like to eat; comment on who in each family drops off and picks up children). |
| *To offer a gentle extension, adults can* | *To offer a gentle extension, adults can* | *To offer a gentle extension, adults can* |
| • Point out that a characteristic a child observes is also shared by one or more other people (e.g., "Karl has black hair. So does Mattie").<br><br>• Talk with children about their families (e.g., what they like to eat, whether they have pets, who is in their family, family routines). | • Help children become aware of a wider variety of characteristics (e.g., make a class photo book and talk about such characteristics as gender, age, hair and skin color, dress, use of adaptive devices).<br><br>• Invite family members to share their interests and traditions with the class (e.g., to bring in music and/or dance with children at large-group time); encourage children to ask the visitors questions about their daily lives or special occasions at home. | • Help children understand that people can be the same in some ways yet different in other ways (e.g., "Moira and Landon both have green eyes, but Moira has red hair and Landon has brown hair").<br><br>• Read books portraying families with different structures and from different backgrounds; post artwork that shows family scenes from different locations and cultures. |

# CHAPTER 4

KDI 54. Community Roles

## H. Social Studies

### 54. Community roles: Children recognize that people have different roles and functions in the community.

**Description:** Children know about familiar roles in the communities they belong to (e.g., family, school, neighborhood). They understand that people depend upon one another. Children know that people need money to buy goods and services.

*At work time in the house area, Joseph, Ella, and Jayla put on fancy dress-up clothes and then "marry each other." Once they are married, they go home (to the block area) and lie down to sleep on pillows covered with blankets.*

*At work time in the block area, Joey makes a McDonald's drive-through window with blocks. He sits inside the structure, takes orders, and passes out food to customers. He uses pink gems as chicken nuggets and Cuisenaire rods as French fries.*

*At work time in the toy area, Kovid makes a "road cleaner" with Lego blocks. He pushes it across the table and explains to his teacher that the roads are dirty from dirty tires. Then he says, "The driver is very careful. He wouldn't want to make a mistake."*

*At greeting time, Jaron announces, "Geneen (his sister) lost another tooth. She put it under her pillow last night and the tooth fairy left her a whole dollar!"*

In their eagerness to act like adults, young children are interested in learning about and imitating grown-up roles and occupations (Gronlund, 2006). Adult roles and responsibilities are a frequent topic of conversation ("My grandma is a teacher"; "When I'm big, I'm gonna drive a digger truck"). They also assume a prominent place in preschoolers' pretend play (the mommy or daddy who buys food and rocks the baby to sleep, the doctor who spoons in medicine and gives shots, the firefighter who puts out the flames after an explosion, or the ice cream lady who dishes out a big scoop in the cup).

## Roles and Responsibilities in and Beyond the Family

As preschoolers explore community roles, they begin by focusing on family members and their responsibilities toward one another. Being naturally self-concerned, young children are initially most preoccupied with actions that involve their well-being, such as who cooks meals, buys toys and clothes, provides comfort when they are sad or sick, or reads them books at bedtime. As they become less egocentric, children are also increasingly aware of the roles family

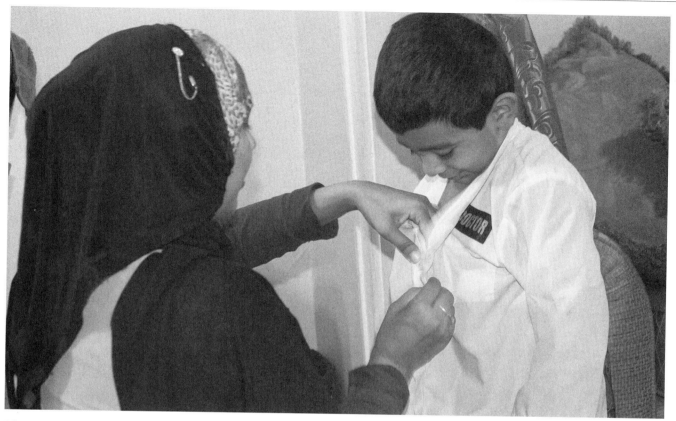

*This child dons a white coat while pretending to be a doctor, a community role that is familiar to him.*

members play outside the home. They become interested in the jobs held by parents and other adults they know, including their relationships with the people at their workplaces (the boss, an office mate). Preschoolers also demonstrate an awareness of other out-of-home but non-job roles (scout leader, hospital volunteer, church choir member, community gardener), although they may not distinguish between paid work and unpaid positions. Finally, young children take a keen interest in non-family service workers with whom they may have varying personal experience. Common pretend-play roles include doctor, firefighter, police officer, teacher, veterinarian, cashier, fix-it person, bus driver, and wait staff.

Preschoolers pay attention not only to *who* these people are but also to *how* they carry out

their duties. They practice skills and acquire specific content knowledge related to a diversity of roles. For example, when children pretend to be a doctor who takes a doll's temperature or gives it a shot, they are demonstrating their emerging awareness of injury or disease and how science treats these conditions. Moreover, in addition to observing the physical attributes of people performing various community roles (their age, gender, or strength), preschoolers are also concerned about the personal qualities of these individuals, such as their kindness, knowledge, or courage.

Young children often see family members and community helpers as heroes and strive to emulate the qualities they depend on and admire. They represent their understanding of who these people are and what they do in their pretend play and artwork, as well as discussing them forthrightly in their conversations with peers and adults. Through their observations and actions, young children form ideas about how society is organized, the variety of roles people play, how adults as well as children depend upon one another, and what they might want to be when they grow up.

## Economics

Young children also begin to develop rudimentary ideas about the nature and uses of money (Jantz & Seefeldt, 1999). While "economics" may seem too abstract a concept to apply to this age group, preschoolers in fact know many things about this domain of social studies from their own experience. For example, they understand that people work to make money to pay for food, clothes, toys, medicine, and other goods and services. Based on their own families, as well as the people they see at preschool and in the community, children know some of the ways people earn a living (for example, in the community roles described above) and the work routines entailed — for example, they know that many people go to work in the morning and come home at dinner time; that they have a boss; that they don't work on the weekend; and that sometimes they have vacations, the same as the children at school do.

Preschoolers also form simple ideas about the mechanics of finance. For example, they know that money comes in various types of currency (paper and coin) but that it can also be represented in other formats such as checks and plastic (credit and debit cards). They understand people can get money at a bank or ATM, although the process might seem magical to them. Observing a financial transaction, for example, they may think the money is "owned" by the bank or the machine, rather than grasp the idea that people are withdrawing funds that belong to them.

*At work time in the house area, Lane shakes her head and says to Becca. "We can't go to the movies. We don't have any money." Becca drapes a purse over her arm and replies, "Let's go to the bank and buy some money." The girls cut pieces of paper in the art area and then return to the house area where they put the "money" on the table and sit down to watch a movie.*

Finally, preschoolers are able to make simple choices about how to spend money. Because they understand at a basic level that money has "value," they consider the "value" of each option when making a decision ("Do I want the toy car or the robot more?"). They also know that some things cost more than others (a computer costs more than a granola bar), although they do not grasp the value of goods and services at an absolute level (that is, the actual cost of and price difference between two objects or services). Nevertheless, in their pretend play, preschoolers will attach monetary value to something and use their emerging sense of number to attach a higher value (a larger number) to convey the relative size or worth of something.

*At greeting time, Jibreel says to his teacher Marion and his classmate Kovid, "If you have money, you can buy bubble gum for everyone."*

*At work time in the house area, Dana is playing waitress, and Maxine and Germaine are her customers. Maxine orders soup, and Dana holds out her hand, saying "That will be eleven-eight cents." When Germaine says he wants soup, pizza, and a plate of cookies, Dana tells him it will cost "a hundred dollars and eleven-eight cents."*

# Teaching Strategies That Support Community Roles

Because preschoolers are inherently interested in the variety of roles played by adults at home and in the community, teachers have many opportunities to support their curiosity and play. To help children learn about community roles, and the social and economic interdependence among people, use the following teaching strategies in your interactions with them.

## Provide opportunities for children to learn about and act out different community roles

Early learning standards in virtually every state recommend that preschools introduce children to different types of jobs and community workers (Gronlund, 2006). For example, the Washington State standards (Kagan, Britto, Kauerz, & Tarrant, 2005) say programs should

- Explain that one person may play different roles (e.g., father and employee).

- Help children distinguish people and relationships (e.g., brother, aunt, cousin).

- Provide opportunities, such as field trips and classroom visitors, for children to see people in different roles.

- Provide opportunities for children to express knowledge of social roles through the arts (e.g., dramatic play, art).

**Family roles and relationships.** As noted above, young children's awareness of roles and the fact that one individual may play more than one role, begins with their families. To help support this emerging realization, talk with children about their family members and what they do inside and outside the home ("Sean's daddy and Mattie's daddy both cooked dinner last night"; "Jerome's aunt is a teacher like me"). Welcome family members into the classroom. Even if parents do not have the time to volunteer or visit during the school day, children can learn a great deal about one another's families during brief routine times such as daily dropoff and pickup. For example, you might mention the jobs family members are going to when they leave in the morning or ask about their work day when they return. Encourage parents who are permitted to bring their children to work now and then to do so, and to create opportunities (at greeting time or snacktime) for children to share these experiences with the rest of the class. Share photos or tell stories about what happened during home visits.

**Field trips and visitors.** Field trips outside the classroom and visitors to the classroom give children firsthand encounters with diverse people in the community and the roles they perform. Plan field trips to various places of work, especially those like the fire station or supermarket that appear spontaneously in children's pretend play. Go to familiar places, such as the library, but instead of just checking out books, focus on what the librarian and other workers do (answering questions by looking up information on the computer, reshelving books and DVDs). As with any field trip, consult with your hosts beforehand to make sure the visit involves active participation and, if possible, bring back materials the children can incorporate into their pretend play (e.g., grocery bags, receipt pads). Recap the experience by writing group thank-you notes in which each child contributes what they liked about the trip, conduct follow-up small-group activities, and provide pretend-play props and art materials for representation.

Trips outside the classroom need not always be formal or involve elaborate arrangements. Even informal walks around the neighborhood allow children to see workers in various roles — the sanitation workers driving their truck and stopping to collect trash and recycling bins at the end of each driveway; the farmers at the farmers' market setting out their wares; shopkeepers putting up signs or creating window displays; and mechanics hoisting cars at the corner garage.

Visitors to the classroom also expand children's ideas about the variety of roles people perform and what is involved in carrying them out. Visitors can include family members sharing their jobs. For example, one preschooler's mother was a clothing designer who brought drawings of her work and fabric scraps for the children. Another child's father was a construction worker, and although his employer thought it was too dangerous to allow children at the worksite, he showed them how to use the construction toys and blocks in the sandbox to excavate and construct an apartment building, and brought old blueprints for the children

to use. This visit resulted in greatly elaborated play in the block area, sand table, and outdoor sandbox. In addition to family members, invite other people from the community to visit the classroom. Again, build on the roles and workplaces children are interested in, and talk with visitors ahead of time about how to make the visit hands-on and appropriate for the children.

**Reading and representation.** Read books that depict not only a variety of family and community roles, but also a diversity of people filling them (see KDI 53. Diversity). For example, read stories and nonfiction books about male nurses and female astronauts. Connect the people and events in the books to children's personal experiences (when you read about Curious George going to the hospital, talk about children's experiences with doctors when they are sick). Sing songs and make up rhymes and

*These children become acquainted with a pizza maker on a field trip to the pizza parlor.*

chants that illustrate various community roles. For example, classics like "Old MacDonald Had a Farm" or "The Wheels on the Bus" open the door to talking about who grows our food or the program's bus or van driver. Encourage children to make up verses to familiar songs that talk about other roles. For example, children can fill in the words and make up actions to "This is the way we…" ("put out the fire," "cook the dinner," "plant the corn").

**Pretend play.** Finally, provide time and materials to encourage children's pretend play as they act out the family and community roles that are meaningful to them. Provide dress-up clothes and props they can incorporate in their play (firefighter helmet, police badge, stethoscope, steering wheel, stamps and notepads). Wherever possible, make these items "real" instead of child-sized play replicas. Encourage children to create additional props with items from the art, house, or block area (a small block can serve as a "microphone" for a rock band, balls can be apples and melons at the fruit stand). Play alongside children as they act out these roles, taking care to let them lead and follow their play themes (see KDI 13. Cooperative play and KDI 43. Pretend play). Make comments and ask occasional questions to help them consider the nature of roles they enact and the people in their lives who fill them. Now and then, add new vocabulary words related to the roles they play.

*At work time in the house area, Lily brings her sick puppy, Paws, to veterinarian Sam (a teacher). Lily is worried because Paws has "monsters" in his tummy. Sam is also worried and says, "We should call an ambulance to take Paws to the dog hospital. They have the right things to fix her there." Lily agrees but wants to make "a bed" for Paws to lie in during the bumpy ambulance ride. Sam explains to Lily, "There's a special bed on wheels, with straps, called a gurney." "Gurney," repeats Lily, "I will make one with the wagon at outside time."*

*At work time in the block area, Tasha puts on the blue coat and says she is a firefighter. She sits in the cardboard box "fire truck" with David. "You be the lady and your house is on fire," Tasha instructs their teacher Emily and points to a nearby table. "Help! My house is on fire," responds Emily, who sits down in a chair. "How will you put out the fire so my house doesn't burn down?" David makes the sound of a siren, and he and Tasha drive (push) the fire truck closer to Emily. "We need a hose," says Tasha and fetches a rope. She tells Emily to get out of the way and squirts water at the table, while David sprays "chemicals" from a large block to which he has taped a pipe cleaner "nozzle." Emily lets the children decide when the fire is "out" so she can safely return home. "You doused the fire with water and chemicals," observes Emily, and thanks them for saving her house from burning down.*

## Provide opportunities for children to learn about and act out relationships that involve exchanging money for goods and services

To help children see how basic economic concepts relate to their own lives, build on everyday experiences to support their growing awareness that goods and services (groceries, movie tickets, and bus rides) are purchased with money or its equivalent. Look for books about stores, shopping, buying and selling, and markets, such as *Maisy Goes Shopping* by Lucy Cousins, *Just Shopping With Mom* by Mercer Mayer, and *Markets* by Cassie Mayer. Join as a play partner as children provide or pay for things at a restaurant, barbershop, or doctor's office. While children enjoy using play money, they also like to cut up strips of paper and use small items (rocks, beads) to pay for the goods and services they buy (pizza, haircuts) as they carry out their play ideas.

*At work time in the house area, Andre pokes a small block a few times and holds it to his ear. "Hello," he says, "I want to order a large pizza with pepperoni. How much will that cost?"*

❖

*At outside time, Felicia drives the big bus and collects a one-dollar "fare" from each of her three riders. The riders pay the fare with one pebble*

*or acorn, which Felicia puts in a small basket. When the teacher asks Felicia what the fare is to ride the bus, Felicia says it will cost her "two dollars." When the teacher comments that the other riders paid one dollar, Felicia explains that "Grown-ups have to pay more than kids because their seats are bigger."*

*At work time in the house area, Jeremy pretends he's a supermarket cashier. He sets out play food on the table, baskets in which the children who are customers can put their purchases, and a small block with squares of paper and pencils. When his teacher asks about the block, papers,*

*While playing "restaurant," children have the opportunity to talk about how much different menu items cost.*

*and pencils, Jeremy explains it is a machine for charge cards and demonstrates how it works. "You rub it along the side and then you sign your name on the top."*

Create opportunities that allow children to recognize the relationship between work and money. For example, when they pretend to carry out the work roles discussed above, make comments and occasionally ask questions to help them understand that people earn money when they perform these jobs ("Doctor, how much do I have to pay you to give my baby a shot?"). As you partner in their play, support their ideas about earning money at work to pay other people for the goods and services they want to buy.

*At work time in the house area, Katie (whose father is a carpenter) says, "I will build a house for John and get some money from him. Then we can go to Disneyland." Her teacher says, "You're going to make money building a house and then we can take a trip to Disneyland."*

For examples of how children at different stages of development express their understanding of community roles, and how adults can support and build on their interests, see "Ideas for Scaffolding KDI 54. Community Roles" on page 42. The chart offers additional suggestions you can use during play and other interactions to scaffold children's understanding in this area.

# Ideas for Scaffolding KDI 54. Community Roles

Always support children at their current level and occasionally offer a gentle extension.

| Earlier | Middle | Later |
|---|---|---|

*Children may*

- Talk about or play family roles (e.g., cook; rock a doll to sleep).
- Engage in simple pretend play that imitates others exchanging goods and services (e.g., when other children play restaurant, also find a token to pay for food; pretend to cut a baby doll's hair when playing barbershop with others).

*Children may*

- Talk about or play community roles they come in direct contact with (e.g., the woman at the bank who gives them a sucker; "We better call Joe [the maintenance person]. The sink is stopped up").
- Pretend to give out goods and services in exchange for money or its equivalent (e.g., play barbershop and say, "It costs a hundred dollars for a haircut"; take tokens to get on the bus).

*Children may*

- Talk about or play less familiar roles and recognize their importance to the community (e.g., "Zoo keepers feed the animals"; "It's good we have garbage collectors or our street would be stinky").
- Show or describe in their play or conversation where money comes from and how people get it (e.g., "I'm the boss. I have all the money"; "My mommy lost her job so I only got one Christmas present").

*To support children's current level, adults can*

- Converse with children about their families; imitate children's actions (e.g., pretend to cook soup on the stove; wash doll clothes in a basin alongside them).
- Provide props that children can use to pretend-play the exchange of goods and services (e.g., poker chips, tokens, pretend money, sample credit cards).

*To support children's current level, adults can*

- Provide clothing and tools for pretend play props (e.g., uniforms, menus); play as partners and follow children's play themes (e.g., when a child says the baby is sick, suggest taking the baby to the doctor).
- Acknowledge that the goods and services children pretend to give you have value; ask how much they cost "How many dollars do I owe you for the shoes?").

*To support children's current level, adults can*

- Ask children to tell them what they need to do to carry out a role when playing the less familiar roles children assign.
- Talk about the fact that people earn money for the work they do (e.g., parents go to work so they can earn money to buy groceries and clothes).

*To offer a gentle extension, adults can*

- Talk with children about the multiple roles played by family members (e.g., "When your mommy leaves here, she teaches at the college. After she picks you up, she takes you home and cooks dinner").
- Label or describe how children exchange goods and services (e.g., "You paid for your French fries").

*To offer a gentle extension, adults can*

- Read books that portray people in various roles, including less common ones (e.g., pilot, archeologist, pharmacist).
- Help children become aware that goods and services vary in value, that is, some have greater monetary worth than others (e.g., "I have enough money to buy one cookie but not the whole box of cookies").

*To offer a gentle extension, adults can*

- Go on field trips and invite visitors to the classroom to acquaint children with a wide variety of community roles.
- Provide props related to money (e.g., price stickers, cash registers, nonfunctional credit card machine, old checkbooks); model how to use them.

# CHAPTER 5

# KDI 55. Decision Making

## H. Social Studies

## 55. Decision making: Children participate in making classroom decisions.

**Description:** Children understand that everyone has the right to share ideas and be heard. They participate as leaders and followers. With adult guidance, they join in class discussions, help make decisions, and share ideas to resolve group problems.

*At snacktime, Monica is absent on the day it is her turn to pass out the cups. The children decide that the person who is next on the list should do it, but that when Monica comes back it will be her turn regardless of whose name is next on the list at that point.*

*As the children head inside at the end of outside time, their teacher comments that some of them almost got hurt when others swung sticks in the air. "Swinging sticks is fun," she says, "but I am worried someone will get hurt. What can we do about this problem?" Gabriel says they shouldn't play with sticks. Nicholas repeats the teacher's statement that swinging sticks is fun. "Kids should swing the sticks down," suggests Bianca. "How would they do that?" asks the teacher, not sure she understands. "Like this," says Bianca, and demonstrates swinging a stick along the ground instead of up in the air. The children like this idea and decide to try it the next day. They invent a "stick game" where they see how many different ways they can swing the stick on the ground. They come up with forward and back, side to side, in circles, and zig-zag.*

Sharing in decision-making is the cornerstone of democracy. Teachers can actively foster an understanding of democratic processes and attitudes when they provide children with concrete opportunities to participate in group decision-making, collaboratively solve problems that arise in the classroom community, express opinions in a group setting, and learn to listen to others' ideas and perspectives (Copple & Bredekamp, 2009). Preschoolers are beginning to learn and accept (with difficulty) that individuals do not always get what they want but that everyone deserves to be heard and have their opinions considered. Moreover, as in resolving social conflicts (KDI 15. Conflict resolution), groups have the capacity to revise decisions if the members feel a solution is not working.

## Making Meaningful Decisions

Educators sometimes use the terms *classroom decisions* and *class rules* interchangeably. However, they are *not* the same thing. *Rules* refers to the limits that adults set for how children should behave ("No hitting or name-calling"; "Don't climb on the bookshelves"; "No running with scissors"; "Don't touch the doorknob"). Although grown-ups appreciate the need for certain rules, rules do not help children develop a capacity for independent decision making. In fact, some rules are more for adults' convenience than for children's well-being.

Rules imposed by adults can seem arbitrary to preschoolers, especially when they are decreed without simple explanations that make sense to a young child. Universal rules — such as posted lists of "do's and don't's" — are abstract. By contrast, decisions about what is safe or healthy at the moment in a particular situation are concrete and personally relevant. Thus, not surprisingly, research shows that when children themselves are included in making decisions, they are not only more likely to go along with them but are also inclined to remind their peers to comply (Elias et al., 1997).

This finding highlights the importance of involving children in making decisions that affect daily classroom life. When classroom decisions are used to solve a particular situation (e.g., people might slip and get hurt if the floor in the block area gets wet), children understand they are solving a health or safety problem. In non-problem situations (e.g., where to store a new material, what to buy for snacktime), they are contributing to the environment in which they live and learn every day.

When preschoolers help to identify group problems or opportunities, generate and agree on solutions, carry out their ideas, and evaluate whether they are working, they are experiencing democracy in action. Of course, decision

*At snacktime, children make decisions about the tasks they will do.*

making can be quite fluid at this age, depending on children's needs or distractions. Impatience may lead to a mid-game shift in the number of turns each player gets, or the finish line of a race may change if the picnic table now looks like a more interesting destination than the tree. Nevertheless, preschoolers are capable of reaching decisions and following through on them when they receive support from adults and are joined by their peers.

As socially motivated beings, young children develop a growing awareness of three types of rules or norms that help people get along in a community (DeVries & Zan, 2003). They understand the need for *health and safety norms* to protect themselves or others (if people run in the classroom, they might fall and hurt themselves or bang into another person and hurt them). Because there are visible (natural) consequences for violating such norms (you ran, you fell, you scraped your knee), these are the easiest ones for young children to accept. With their growing capacity for empathy, preschoolers can also begin to appreciate *moral norms,* the purpose of which is to treat others fairly and with respect. Finally, young children grasp the usefulness of *discretionary norms* for sharing responsibilities or resolving conflicts. They also realize these can be changed by mutual agreement of the group (e.g., "We normally have one person pass out the cups, but today Ella agreed that Sarah could help her").

# The Roots of Participatory Decision Making

The development of certain social-emotional skills, notably the capacity for self-regulation and empathy, allows preschoolers to participate in the decision-making process. They can balance their own needs and preferences against those of others, and are acquiring the cognitive and social flexibility to see things from more than one perspective (Harter, 1999, 2006). Preschoolers are also shifting from regarding themselves solely as individuals to identifying themselves as group members too. As such, they strive to make the group work better to achieve both personal and shared goals (Thompson, 2006).

For example, preschoolers who see themselves as members of a community recognize the need to take care of the classroom equipment and materials. They understand that if someone rips the pages out of a book, then no one can read the whole story, and that if they forget to put the tops on the markers, the markers will dry out and no one can draw a picture with them. As children increasingly pay attention to cause and effect, they are also capable of identifying communal problems as well as offering solutions. The following discussion, which took place one day at greeting time, was a perfect opportunity for participatory decision making:

**Carlson:** Cleanup takes so long, we don't have a lot of time to play outside.

**Simone:** We should clean up faster!

**Teacher:** How can we do that?

**Brett:** Let's work in table groups and see if we can beat the timer!

**Carlson:** Sue's table can work in the block area, and Jose's group can work in the house area. Then when we finish, we go to another area.

**Simone:** We could start cleanup sooner.

**Brett:** Yeah! But then work time wouldn't be as long.

**Simone:** You're right. I don't want to do that. I want to do the timer.

**Teacher:** So the idea is to split into table groups and use a timer? *(The children nod yes.)* Should we use the sand timer or the kitchen timer?

**Brett:** If we use the kitchen timer, we can hear the bell!

**Teacher:** Okay, then. We can race the kitchen timer and see if we can clean up faster?

**Brett:** Yeah!

**Teacher:** I think you all solved the problem. Let's give it a try tomorrow.

Decision making is not only about solving problems, however. There are also opportunities that children can decide together. For example, they may decide where to go on a field trip, in what area of the classroom to store a new piece of equipment, which song(s) to sing at large-group time, how to celebrate the return of a teacher who has been absent a long time, or how to invite the custodian to show them how she mops the floors. Being an active participant in making these decisions cements children's sense of community — their commitment to and ownership of the classroom. It also promotes initiative (KDI 1. Initiative) and contributes to children's sense of competence (KDI 8. Sense of competence). Children learn to see themselves as capable individuals who can influence the course of events.

## The Development of Decision Making

Young children invited to contribute to classroom decisions exhibit the following developmental progression (DeVries & Zan, 2003):

**Parroting or repeating others' ideas.** Children who do not yet know their opinions matter, especially if they are new to participatory decision making, tend to merely repeat or agree with what others say. Young preschoolers may also not fully appreciate the topic being discussed, or may lack the cognitive and verbal skills to formulate and express their ideas.

*Children in this group decide how they will take turns adding their pieces to the puzzle.*

*At the end of small-group time, when the teacher asks where to store the large cardboard boxes, Dylan repeats "block area" after Sean suggests putting them there. But when Marnie replies, "Let's put them in the house area to use as dog houses," Dylan looks confused and then agrees by saying "house area." When the teacher asks him, "Dylan, do you think we should put the boxes in the block area or the house area?" he shrugs his shoulders.*

**Elaborating on others' ideas.** Although these contributions are not wholly the child's creation, they reflect a growing sense of autonomy and power. Just as preschoolers develop the capacity to build on one another's play ideas, so too do they increasingly listen to and elaborate on the ideas of their peers in group decision-making settings. They make concrete suggestions that often combine or vary those offered by their peers, as seen in the continuation of the above scenario:

*Zoe suggests, "We could put some boxes in the block area and some boxes in the house area!" Sean, Marnie, and Dylan all agree this is a good idea.*

**Inventing original ideas.** Contributing new ideas reflects children's growing ability to think about the matter under discussion and imagine (mentally represent) how their suggestion will play out. It also involves having the words to express their thoughts so that others can understand and respond to them. Finally, offering original contributions grows out of children's cumulative experience with the decision-making process itself. By this point, they have learned that their opinions are welcomed and will be given fair consideration by the group.

*At greeting time, the teacher draws a stick figure and tells the children that tomorrow a new girl named Ella will be joining the class. "If she sits next to me, I will show her how to pour juice," says Janie. "Ella's cubby can be next to mine because it's empty," offers Max. "Does she like to roll in the snow?" asks Georgia. "Let's make a card and write 'Hi Ella' on it," suggests Joey. Making the card becomes Joey's plan, and after he completes it at work time, several other children write their names or letter links on it.*

You may recognize the progression described above as you think about all the times during the daily routine when children make decisions for themselves, such as at planning time or large-group time. For example, they may begin by repeating someone's else's idea (when the first two children at the table plan to go to the block area, Latoya points to the block area too). Later, they may decide on a variation (after Jamie pats his nose to the music at large-group time, Dov pats his cheek when it's his turn to make a suggestion). Finally, children begin to come up with wholly original ideas (Mark plans to go to the block area and build a fire station, while Tanya says she's going to play the shape game at the computer; Flo chooses to pat her elbow, while Eddie bends to touch his toes).

# Teaching Strategies That Support Decision Making

Participating in group decisions helps children become citizens of the classroom. It builds their understanding of social processes and solidifies their membership in the community. As they take steps toward assuming responsibility for others as well as themselves, children simultaneously develop a sense of independence and belonging. To help them make decisions with personal confidence while respecting the equality of their peers, use the following teaching strategies.

## Provide opportunities for children to solve problems and make plans as a group

Just as children need practice making choices to develop their initiative as individuals (KDI 1. Initiative), so too do they need repeated experiences to become effective group decision makers. Multiple opportunities allow them to develop skills such as listening, contributing, reflecting, respecting, anticipating, and evaluating. Decision-making opportunities, when facilitated by patient and supportive adults, also build children's self-confidence by showing that their opinions count.

**Keep decision-making matters simple.** Begin by offering simple matters to decide, such as where to post the list for passing out cups and napkins. Greeting time provides an opportunity to present the problem and open a discussion. Make sure all the children understand the problem or opportunity being discussed, and clarify the options and any limits or boundaries that apply ("It has to be low enough for everyone to see"). At first, you might suggest two or three choices. Later, once preschoolers become more adept at making decisions, encourage them to generate possible options as well as voice their preferences. As with other problem-solving activities, encourage children to consider more than one alternative or option as they generate ideas and choose solutions. Ask questions such as, "What do you think would happen if…?" and "Is there another way we could try to do that?"

**Create a safe environment.** Because group decision making is like other shared activities in which children take risks (such as expressing feelings, sharing opinions about artwork, offering explanations and hypotheses), it is important to create a safe emotional and physical environment surrounding the process. A safe classroom climate supports the free and respectful exchange of feelings and ideas. Help children listen to one another by modeling attentive and respectful listening yourself. When necessary, repeat or restate children's ideas so the others can understand them. Encourage children to help one another remember and carry out the group's decisions. Just as children are more apt to examine their mathematical or scientific thinking when questioned by other children, they may be more apt to follow through on a decision when reminded and helped by a peer than an adult.

**Anticipate problems.** Where possible, anticipate group problems or identify them early in the process before emotions run high and patterns of behavior are firmly established (Gartrell, 2006). For low-key problems (children creating a slippery surface by dripping water on the floor as they carry cups of water from the sink to the house area), you can involve the children concerned in making a decision on the spot. For more emotional decisions (what to do about children excluding others from play), it is often best to wait until a calmer time to raise the matter. For more on conflict resolution techniques to facilitate group discussion and joint decision making, see KDI 15. Conflict resolution, in *Social and Emotional Development* (Epstein, 2012).

**Use decisions to create opportunities as well as to solve problems.** Remember that decisions apply to creating and planning group opportunities as well as to solving classroom problems. Whenever possible, involve children in making "positive" decisions, such as where to store new equipment and materials in the classroom, which direction to turn during a neighborhood walk, what containers to use to sort a collection, and how to thank a visitor or host. Don't offer children false opportunities or unrealistic choices (e.g., for snack items that are not within your budget or field-trip destinations that are too far away). Rather than empowering children and boosting their self-confidence,

*Children gain confidence when adults support them in trying out their ideas and decisions.*

these may lead children to grow distrustful or feel their ideas carry no weight.

**Try out children's ideas.** In a similar vein of validating children's importance and· relevance in the decision-making process, commit yourself to trying out their ideas. This includes impractical ones, as long as they are not physically or emotionally dangerous or beyond the program's resources. Children will learn more about the decision making process by experiencing the outcome firsthand, rather than having an adult tell them their ideas will not work out. You may even be surprised to discover that the decision the children reach works better than one you thought of yourself! The following from Ann Epstein (2009) illustrates how children in one classroom made some decisions.

*The class has recently begun recycling paper and containers in bins provided by the city. Many families take part in the municipal recycling program at home as well. The children have been talking about why it is good to reuse things and not waste them. The following conversation takes place one day at the end of snack time:*

"**Teacher:** Jonathan, can you please throw away the empty cereal box? *(Pointing to the trash can)*

**Giselle:** We don't have to throw it away, Mrs. Conte. We could use it in the art area.

**Teacher:** What could we do with it?

**Giselle:** Cut it up and use it as a recyclable to make something or for decorations.

**Raquel:** And this empty yogurt cup. *(It had been washed clean.)* I want to use it.

**Teacher:** How will you use it?

**Raquel:** To mix paint in.

**Giselle:** I can bring in more yogurt cups from home. Raquel and I will do a project together" (p. 135).

**Evaluate decisions.** Finally, involve the children in evaluating the success of group decisions. Help them ask and answer the following questions: Did our idea solve the problem ("Is the floor in the house area drier so children will not slip")? Did our decision about how to proceed meet our goals ("Did writing a note encourage the janitor to let us try the big mops")? Do we want to continue the policy ("Should we still have one person pass out the cups or should two children share the task")? Should we do something we enjoyed again ("Would you like to go back to the farmers market")? Do we need to make a different decision and see if that works better ("Callie can't see the chore chart from her wheelchair. Where else could we hang it")? Did the decision work so well that we want to expand on it ("What other workers should we invite to show us how they do their job")?

## Encourage children to consider how their choices and decisions affect others

Support children as they begin to understand how group decisions affect classroom cooperation and interdependence. Encourage them to pay attention to the outcomes of the decision-making process. Acknowledge when a decision has added to the classroom's efficiency ("Since we decided to race the timer at cleanup time, we've been able to play outside longer"), enjoyment ("By turning down this street, we got to see the bulldozers"), or sense of camaraderie ("We felt proud of ourselves when we wrote the thank you letter to Mr. Haley"). Likewise, help raise children's awareness of any unintended negative effects of a group decision ("No one is using the small boxes since we moved them to the block area. Where else could we put them so we remember they are available for work time?"). When children realize their choices affect others, they can choose to use their decision-making skills for the good of the community.

For examples of how children demonstrate their decision-making capabilities and how adults can support and extend their learning step by step, see "Ideas for Scaffolding KDI 55. Decision Making" on page 52. The chart presents more ideas for carrying out the strategies detailed above as you play and interact with the children in your program.

# Ideas for Scaffolding KDI 55. Decision Making

Always support children at their current level and occasionally offer a gentle extension.

| Earlier | Middle | Later |
|---|---|---|
| *Children may* | *Children may* | *Children may* |
| • Talk over or be distracted when others are sharing their ideas. | • Listen to another person share his or her idea(s); may repeat the other person's idea (e.g., after another child suggests taking turns, say, "I know! Let's take turns!"). | • Acknowledge what others say by building on their ideas (e.g., "Yeah! We could plant tomatoes, and I want to plant beans too!"). |
| • Not offer ideas or make statements unrelated to the topic being decided (e.g., When deciding where to go on a class walk, say, "Trucks!"). | • Offer ideas related to the topic being decided that may be general or may not be practical or safe (e.g., "Everybody should share!"; "We could buy more computers"). | • Offer ideas related to the topic being decided that are specific, practical, and/or safe (e.g., "If someone is hiding under the table at cleanup time, tell them to help put away the toys"; "We should put a 'NO' sign on the climber so we remember it's too icy to play on"). |
| *To support children's current level, adults can* | *To support children's current level, adults can* | *To support children's current level, adults can* |
| • Accept when children are not interested in being part of a decision-making discussion. | • Repeat children's ideas even though they've already been stated by someone else. | • Acknowledge when children listen and build on one another's ideas (e.g., "When Mikko said we could take turns, you thought we could do that by using the sand timer"). |
| • Acknowledge children's statements even if they are unrelated to the topic under discussion (e.g., "Gerry says trucks"). | • Restate or rephrase children's ideas even if they are vague or not practical (e.g., "Maya's idea is to share the computer"). | • Explain how and why a child's idea will work (e.g., "Telling someone to put away the toys at cleanup time *would* help remind them what to do"). |
| *To offer a gentle extension, adults can* | *To offer a gentle extension, adults can* | *To offer a gentle extension, adults can* |
| • Repeat ideas to help children attend and listen to them (e.g., "Daryl's idea is to name the guinea pig Sniffy"). | • Point out when a child's idea is the same as another child's idea (e.g., "Uri said we should use towels. You have the same idea"). | • Summarize the ideas children offer (verbally or on a list) and ask them if you've forgotten any. |
| • Comment on others' ideas that are related to the topic (e.g., "Rollo wants the class to walk to the nature trail"); do not criticize or say that a child's statement is unrelated to the topic. | • Ask children to describe their ideas in more detail (e.g., "Kelly, your idea is that everybody should share the xylophone. How can we do that?"). | • Encourage children to elaborate further on how to carry out their ideas (e.g., "Where would we get the towels to wipe up the spills?"); brainstorm possible barriers and solutions (e.g., "We don't have money to buy a lot more towels. How else could we get towels?"). |

# CHAPTER 6

# KDI 56. Geography

**H. Social Studies**

## 56. Geography: Children recognize and interpret features and locations in their environment.

. . . . . . . . . . . . . . . . . . . . . . . . . . . . . . . . . . . . . . . . . . . .

**Description:** Children identify familiar landmarks (e.g., home, school, park) and navigate simple routes between them. They match objects and events to their locations (e.g., scissors/art area; outside time/playground) and represent physical features (e.g., buildings, roads, bridges) in their play. Children use simple maps to describe and locate things in their environment (e.g., classroom areas, playground features).

*At snacktime, Gabe announces, "Thai lives down the block from me. I can walk to his house"*

*At greeting time, Mikey arrives late but excited. "There was a big accident. My dad and me had to drive all the way around the park to get to school!"*

*At work time in the block area, Ben and Nomi build a farm with a barn for cows and a "riding corral" for horses. They spread sheets of paper for the fields. Nomi milks (squeezes) the toy cows, while Ben drives a truck on the "road that goes all the way around the farm."*

*At work time in the art area, Senguele, Tasha, and Sue (their teacher) talk about the movie "Madagascar." Senguele explains, "Madagascar is a kind of Africa. There are trees with coconuts on them. There's penguins and a king."*

Although "geography" sounds like an abstract subject for preschoolers, early childhood education is quite compatible with its definition as stated in the Geography Education Standards Project (1994): "A field of study that enables us to find answers to questions about the world around us — about where things are and how and why they got there" (p. 11). Given that preschoolers ask these types of questions, geography is an appropriate area of early social studies learning.

## Young Children and Geography

Young children are naturally inquisitive about the places where they live and learn. As their awareness of their surroundings grows, they consciously orient themselves in space and begin to see objects and the environment where they are located from more than one perspective. This ability to see multiple viewpoints has both cognitive advantages (it aids problem-solving) and social benefits (it builds empathy). Getting the "lay of the land" in their own communities or other familiar places (such as the neighborhood where a grandparent lives) creates the foundation for geography studies of expanding regions later in school.

Geography concepts like city, state, or country hold little meaning for young children, although they can be taught to parrot such words in the same way they mechanically recite ABC or 1-2-3. However, as preschoolers' boundaries widen from home to block to neighborhood to cross-town and possibly to faraway locations to visit family or take vacations, they understand in a very real way that there is a vast world beyond their immediate experience. Likewise, encounters with different terrains and geographical features — city to suburb to countryside, sidewalk to park to forest, stream to river to ocean — raise children's awareness that the world consists of a variety of environments. They recognize that each has distinctive natural features (boulders, trees, sand) and human-made forms (buildings, roads, bridges). Preschoolers are eager to discover and learn about all these settings, and to incorporate them in their artistic representations and pretend play.

The challenge for educators is identifying and introducing young children to the key geography concepts that do have meaning and interest for them. As early as 1934, Lucy Sprague Mitchell's influential book *Young Geographers* emphasized the need to build on the "here-and-now" world of preschoolers to expand their understanding of the near and far universe. Using our knowledge of early development, we can identify three promising areas for early geography learning in preschool (Jantz & Seefeldt, 1999): spatial systems (simple mapping), places and regions (familiar locations), and physical systems (the earth's natural features).

*Young children are naturally inquisitive about the places where they live and learn.*

# Simple Mapping

**Spatial awareness.** As noted under mathematics, spatial awareness (KDI 35. Spatial awareness) expands rapidly during the preschool years. Research shows that mapping abilities develop sooner than Piaget and other cognitive theorists originally thought (Liben & Downs, 1993). For example, children as young as three spontaneously draw or build maps. In a cross-national study, preschoolers shown an aerial photo map of their neighborhood were able to plot a route from one familiar point to another (Blades, 1998). Young children's ability to use aerial maps improves when adults first scaffold their learning by pointing out familiar landmarks and encouraging them to trace paths between them with their fingers or drawing tools (Plester, 2002). Building on their here-and-now world enables children to extend their spatial thinking to places beyond their firsthand experience.

**More flexible thinking.** Between the ages of four and five, children reach a level of flexibility in their thinking that lets them see a map and consider a spatial problem from more than one perspective (Vasilyeva, 2002). Younger children can only use a map if it is oriented to their position and they are asked to locate a place or find an object on it for themselves. By contrast, the older children can begin to consider how a map looks to someone seated opposite or perpendicular to them, and how that other person would have to move to be in that place or retrieve the object. Thus, the perspective taking that allows children to solve problems with materials and peers also helps them acquire simple concepts in geography.

**Use of geometric properties.** Children aged three to five are also increasingly able to use the geometric properties of space, not just landmarks, to locate objects (Liben & Yekel, 1996). For example, Gouteux (2001) found that when asked to find an object that they saw an adult hide, younger children oriented themselves using familiar landmarks (e.g., they remembered the object was near a table), while older children oriented themselves and objects in relation to one another (e.g., they remembered the object was on the shelf behind the table closest to the door). In the absence of any landmarks (an object hidden in one of several rectangles, which are then shifted out of children's sight before they are asked to choose the one with the object), only older preschoolers were able to use the rectangle's dimensions as a clue to choose the correct hiding place (Vasilyeva, 2006).

**Maps of open space.** Finally, preschoolers are able to increasingly use a map of an open space, such as a field, to find a hidden (buried) object marked with an "X" on the map. As their spatial sense develops, children can use information about where the object is located based on its position from the sides and corners of the field (Stea, Kirkman, Pinon, Middlebrook, & Rice, 2004). From these findings, it is clear that geography in social studies and spatial awareness in mathematics are closely linked. Children learn by working with objects as well as navigating themselves through space.

# Familiar Locations

Young children are like explorers and civil engineers. They dig in the sand to construct hills and tunnels, investigate how water moves and affects the surrounding terrain, create rock formations to see what makes them balance or collapse, and observe the contrasting conditions that allow different types of plants and animals to live. Given their curiosity, preschoolers are ready to be introduced to basic location or place concepts in geography.

### Experiences inform understanding.

Young children can learn "place geography" if their own experiences serve as the springboard (Mayer, 1995). For example, they can begin with what they know about the terrain or climate where they live to understand there are environments that are different ("Where I live there are mountains and it gets cold and snows. My grandma lives next to a huge ocean with sunny beaches"). That is why books like *The Snowy Day* by Ezra Jack Keats appeal to children in warm weather climates and rural landscapes as much as to children living in northern urban settings. Using their emerging classification skills, preschoolers can organize this place information to compare and contrast the characteristics of geographical regions they have not directly observed.

### Beliefs affect understanding.

Preschool children's understanding of place is also affected by their beliefs about the natural and physical world (KDI 51. Natural and physical world). For example, they attribute life and consciousness to inanimate objects such as the sun, moon, stars, and clouds, as well as to moving bodies of water and even vehicles (Jantz & Seefeldt, 1999). They also retain the belief that geographical features exist for a purpose that they can relate to (mountains exist for climbing, lakes exist for swimming or boating). While the thinking behind these ideas is technically "wrong," attaching human purposes to natural features allows young children to ally with and take an interest in them. They can use knowledge about their own needs and movements to understand how the geographical landscape functions. For example, water moves around obstacles in its path. It takes more energy to go up than down.

*Given their interest in shoveling gravel, these preschoolers are ready to be introduced to basic concepts about geographical features.*

# Natural Features

The study of natural features involves learning about the earth's atmosphere, how the earth's surface is shaped by physical processes, and how the sun affects conditions on earth. These concepts sound very abstract for preschoolers — who may believe the moon follows them around at night! Nevertheless, young children are capable of developing simple ideas about the universe through their own concrete experiences of day and night, shadows, and seasons.

For example, preschoolers are genuinely curious about the weather and often make spontaneous observations about it (Huffman, 1996). A daily chart with a "weather report" will *not* make sense to them, but they do care about how the weather affects their ability to go outside, how seasons determine what outdoor clothing they wear, and how natural conditions such as sunshine and rainfall influence the growth rate of the lettuce they plant in the class garden.

Likewise, children may enjoy looking at cloud formations and movements, or (if they live on the water) observing tidal patterns. Children whose parents' work is tied to climate conditions (for example, farmers and fishermen) may be especially attuned to them. Rainbows often hold as much fascination for children as they do for adults, and young scientists may experiment with prisms, water, mirrors, and other equipment to duplicate the conditions that create them. In short, when children study these phenomena in relation to their own lives, they "behave very much like geographers, not only investigating their world and learning facts but also, more importantly, relating each fact to others and forming generalizations" (Jantz & Seefeldt, 1999, p. 173). The study of geography then takes on very concrete meaning to young children.

# Teaching Strategies That Support Geography

The study of geography in early childhood is closely aligned with preschoolers' curiosity about their expanding experiences in natural and human-made environments. Young children take an interest in the location of familiar landmarks, the physical features of different terrains, and the lives of people who inhabit surroundings that are similar to as well as different from their own. To promote children's early explorations in geography, use the following teaching strategies.

### Acquaint children with familiar locations in their community

Raise children's awareness of places in their community, such as homes, schools, parks, libraries, stores, restaurants, movie theaters, mailboxes, and other locations they and their families visit. Hold conversations about where and how they travel between these familiar places. For example, encourage children to describe their trip to school each day, including the mode of transportation they used and places they passed along the way. If they take an alternate route — perhaps because they slept at grandma's house last night or the car was in for repair and they took the bus — talk about what they experienced that was different (unfamiliar streets; using a pass card on the bus) and/or the same (they still passed the house with the red door just before reaching the school building).

Encourage children to talk about travels with their families, whether going by car or plane to visit relatives, going on a picnic or trip to an amusement park, or taking a vacation in a different part of the country. Provide opportunities for them to represent these experiences in their artwork and pretend play. Talk with children about what they saw; the more you encourage

*These children learn about different ecosystems during their field trip to a local botanical garden.*

them to reflect on and describe these experiences, the more detail they will include in their representations. Invite families to bring in photos of these experiences and post them where other children and their parents can see them. Create a book of all the places children in the program have visited.

*At work time in the house area, the twins Simon and Sybil act out the camping trip they took with their family. They drape a large sheet over the table for a tent and curl up in blankets they call*

*"sleeping bags." Over the course of several days, other children get interested in their pretend play scenario. The twins' parents bring in a cookstove and a lantern to expand the children's play. One day at large-group time, the teacher turns out the lights and the children use flashlights to go on a nighttime hike around the "mountains" and "lakes" in the room.*

Take walks in the school building to locate the front door, office, older children's classrooms, kitchen, teachers' lounge, and other locations that are meaningful to the children. Walk around the neighborhood and point out familiar landmarks and interesting places ("That's where Lila and her dad ate breakfast before school today"; "Tomorrow is my sister's birthday. I'm going to buy her cupcakes at this shop"). Stop at familiar places and encourage children to orient their bodies or point toward home base (the school). Draw simple maps and encourage children to draw simple maps and locate familiar places on them with symbols, flags, stickers, or other markers.

*At recall time, Gracie uses a map of the room to say where she played and what materials she used. She puts her finger in the house area and says, "I cooked spaghetti at the stove. I got water at the sink [she moves her finger to where the sink is marked on the map] and carried it all the way back without spilling" (she slides her finger back to the house area).*

*At outside time, the children and teachers walk three blocks to the farmers' market. En route, the children point to familiar places: the park, McDonald's, and the public library. On the way back, Todd says, "I bet we're gonna see the school when we go around this corner."*

### Use concrete representations to connect children to places beyond their own experience

Books and stories, photographs, artwork, songs, puzzles, and other concrete representations can help young children become aware that there are people and places beyond those they encounter in their own lives. By connecting what they see and hear in these sources to matters of interest to them — what people eat and wear, what their homes look like, where children play and the toys they play with, what animals families keep as pets — you can create many opportunities for preschoolers to investigate lives and experiences that both parallel and differ from their own.

For example, read and encourage children to draw a map of or reenact *Rosie's Walk* by Pat Hutchins. This allows them to construct a "mental map" of her travels across the barnyard, as well as helping children think about various locations on a farm (a valuable challenge for children raised in the city). Bring in books, photographs, and reproductions of paintings and sculptures depicting other places, especially those that feature different styles of clothing, architecture, and other visible characteristics of life elsewhere. Think of the things that interest young children in their own lives (family members, pets, toys and games, clothing, food, words) and find ways to share these same objects and practices in other locations in the United States and abroad.

*Books and other concrete representations can help children learn about people and places beyond those they see in their everyday lives.*

*At work time in the book area, Eli looks at a book of photographs from Morocco. He points to the minarets and tells his teacher, "These roofs are round like a circle. My house is pointy like a triangle." Later, in the block area, he builds a house, balancing the half-circle block on top.*

❖

*At large-group time, Nicu's mother teaches the class a Romanian folk song about digging and roasting potatoes. Following the words of the song, the children "harvest" the potatoes with spoons and then cradle them in their arms to "cook" them. Nicu's mother leaves behind a book with pictures of Nicu's grandparents on their potato farm in Romania.*

Preschoolers are also increasingly interested in looking at road and contour maps, globes, aerial photographs, and compasses. To keep these geography materials from being abstract, connect them with the children's personal experiences. For example, if you are reading a story set in the far north like the *Three Snow Bears* by Jan Brett, compare the clothing the children wear to keep warm with the garments worn by characters in the book. Talk about different elevations children encounter every day (the hill in the schoolyard) or other landscape features (the river that winds through town) as you look at photos of other locations with similar features.

*At outside time, after seeing the movie* Polar Express *with their families, Bradley and Leo pretend they are going to the North Pole. They invite their teacher to join them. She asks what clothing she should pack to stay warm. Bradley suggests boots, and Leo says mittens and a "furry wooly hat." Bradley says they need a big sled to get across the ice. "Don't put too many people or toys on it," warns Leo, "or it might crack and sink down!"*

*Verna and Richard pretend to be pirates on a ship they build with large hollow blocks. They decide to look for buried treasure using a treasure map (road map) from the book area. Verna spreads out the map and gives directions. "That way," she says, pointing toward the toy area. Richard holds a telescope (an empty paper towel tube) to his eye to look in that direction.*

For examples of how children demonstrate their understanding of geography at different stages of development and how adults can support and gradually expand their learning, see "Ideas for Scaffolding KDI 56. Geography" on page 62. Use the additional ideas in the chart to scaffold early geography learning throughout your play and other interactions with preschool children.

# Ideas for Scaffolding KDI 56. Geography

Always support children at their current level and occasionally offer a gentle extension.

| Earlier | Middle | Later |
|---------|--------|-------|
| *Children may* | *Children may* | *Children may* |
| • Match or locate specific objects and events in their immediate environment, such as their home or school (e.g., go to their table for planning time; "The bike goes in the shed"). <br><br> • Identify labels and area signs in the classroom (e.g., put tape on the shelf with the tape label and say, "It goes here"; at planning time, point to the "block area" card and go to that area to play). | • Identify characteristics and landmarks in familiar neighborhoods (e.g., "My grandma has a big lake with freighters"; "To go home, we take the bus and get off at the McDonald's sign"). <br><br> • Read a simple, familiar diagram or map, such as a map of the classroom (e.g., find the block area on the map and put a figure there to show that's where they played at work time). | • Identify characteristics and landmarks in familiar communities (e.g., "For a special treat, my daddy drives me to the ice cream store next to Home Depot"). <br><br> • Read a simple, unfamiliar diagram or map, such as a diagram of the park (e.g., figure out where to feed the ducks on a teacher-drawn diagram; play a computer game involving finding hidden treasure on a map). |
| *To support children's current level, adults can* | *To support children's current level, adults can* | *To support children's current level, adults can* |
| • Label materials and be consistent about where events in the daily routine occur so children become aware of where things belong and where activities happen. <br><br> • Provide opportunities for children to refer to labels and signs (e.g., use area signs at planning and recall; ask children to point to where they think something drawn or written on the message board is located). | • Show interest when children talk about places their families live and visit (e.g., "Your grandma lives on a lake and you see the freighters when you visit her"); ask what they see on the way to familiar places in their neighborhoods. <br><br> • Use simple maps (e.g., classroom map at planning and recall time; a map with an "X" on the message board in the area where a new material is located). | • Talk about landmarks familiar to the children (e.g., "At the mall, I go to the toy store across from the fountain"; "I live next door to the library"). <br><br> • Provide diagrams and maps throughout the classroom (e.g., simple diagrams to build things in the block area; road maps and atlases in the book or house area; computer games with maps to locate hidden objects). |
| *To offer a gentle extension, adults can* | *To offer a gentle extension, adults can* | *To offer a gentle extension, adults can* |
| • Converse with children about where objects are located and where events take place in familiar but nonimmediate environments (e.g., at snacktime, talk about which room they watch television in at home). <br><br> • Ask children to help locate objects in the environment (e.g., at cleanup time, ask where to put something away; involve children in deciding where in the room to locate new materials or equipment). | • Help children become familiar with other nearby neighborhoods (e.g., take a walk near the school and encourage children to anticipate what they might see — post office, gas station, fruit stand — and play I spy, sighting those landmarks). <br><br> • Encourage children to add one or two details to simple maps (e.g., at recall time, ask children to mark the location of a material they used in an area where they played). | • Observe similarities and differences between children's own and other neighborhoods (e.g., on a field trip, say "That looks like our playground. I wonder if we'll see a flower shop too"). <br><br> • Provide materials and opportunities for children to represent experiences using simple maps and diagrams (e.g., drawing and building materials to represent the landmarks in their neighborhoods or places they visit with their families). |

# KDI 57. History

**H. Social Studies**
**57. History:** Children understand past, present, and future.

**Description:** Children talk about what happened in the past (e.g., "Yesterday, when I was a baby…") and what will occur in the future ("When I'm bigger, I'll go to my sister's school"). They describe a sequence of events ("First I painted a picture, and then I built a tower").

*At greeting time, Penny announces, "Last night my dad and me went to the hockey game."*

*At snacktime, Raoul says, "The next time we have trail mix, let's add more pretzels. They're my favorite."*

*At work time in the book area, while looking at a book about Abraham Lincoln, Daniel observes, "He wore a really tall hat." He goes to the art area and makes a tall hat for himself.*

*At outside time, Rachel and Flynn make "light guns" with long cardboard tubes and ride "spaceship" tricycles to "Planet Bingo." When they get there, they build fires with sticks to keep warm. Rachel explains, "Planet Bingo is really cold because it's far away from the sun."*

*At recall time, Terra says, "I went to the water table to mix red and blue water. Then Julius asked me to help him make a hair shop. That took a long time because we had to build it first, and then we had a lot of customers. After that I wanted to paint, but it was time to clean up."*

History, like geography, is an appropriate area of study for preschoolers when it is aimed at "helping children understand the richness and variety of people's lived experiences in different times and places" (Barton & Levstik, 1996, p. 444). To make the study of history meaningful to young children, their present experiences can be used to help them think about what came before ("Once upon a time…") and what might happen in the future ("When I grow up…"). These connections will make their explorations of history real and concrete.

## How Young Children Understand History

Children are most interested in their own past. Their favorite stories, pictures and movies will usually be the ones in which they star, and they will request them over and over again. From this personal fascination grows an interest in where they fit into the wider world. It begins with their immediate families ("Why is baby Lissa here? When is she going back?") and expands to include their schools and community ("Will preschool still be here when I go to kindergarten?"; "My daddy says those tracks are really, really old").

For preschoolers, history *is* all about "the story" (Egan, 1997; Levstik, 1986). They understand the progression of time in the same way they process any narrative: first this happened, then that happened, and so on. Each event in the historical narrative involves characters, settings, actions, and outcomes. It is the people and what happens to them that gives history its meaning and personal relevance. In this way, children are like many adults for whom history comes alive through storytelling (in biography and historical novels) that recreates past events in vivid scenes and dialogue. Also, with children as with adults, it is important that historical narratives not convey misinformation or promote gender and cultural stereotypes (Seefeldt, 1993).

Young children often come to school with a greater awareness of history than we realize (Barton, 1997). Not surprisingly, their knowledge is more about social than political or economic history, and derives from contacts in their everyday lives — artifacts, places, pictures, and oral traditions passed down through families (e.g., a grandparent's rotary dial telephone, a photo of their house before the apartment building went up next door, or a farmer carrying produce to market in a horse-drawn wagon). This social awareness of how people lived in the past provides a foundation upon which children can effectively build an understanding of historical principles.

## The Early Development of Historical Concepts

**Cognitive development.** Children's ideas about history are closely related to their cognitive development, notably their conception of time (Wyner & Farquhar, 1991). At first the perception of time is personal and intuitive (Barry-Davis, 1999). Children associate time with the order and length of events in their own experiences, especially the cycle of daily events:

*At snacktime, Paula says, "My daddy will be gone for three more sleeps. Then he will come back home."*

❖

*Mark, a five-year old, was asked, "How long is a day?" He replied, "It's today until you get to tomorrow!" He was then asked, "How long is that?" Mark replied, 'Today is when you get up and you play and you eat lunch and you play some more and you go to school and you come home and it's nice outside and then it's night and you go to sleep and when you wake up it's tomorrow!"* (Jantz, 1976, p. 96).

*Children like to share stories and hear stories from adults about themselves again and again.*

By late preschool, however, children also begin to apply logic to understanding time. They are aware that time moves forward, and can therefore reason backward (use "reversibility thinking") to construct what happened before. That is, they enjoy hearing stories about when they were born, and what they did as babies and toddlers. They begin to see how the recent past affects the present (they bought a new jacket over the weekend; now they get to wear it to school on Monday). As their ability to represent things continues to grow, preschoolers can stretch further back into that past to connect it with current events (Povinelli, Landry, Theall, Clark, & Castille, 1999).

**Vocabulary development.** A growing vocabulary also helps preschoolers develop a sense of time (Thornton & Vukelich, 1988). Although shaky on specifics, preschoolers eventually grasp through repeated experiences with these time concepts that a minute is shorter than an hour, and a day is shorter than a year. Thus, when they hear about something that occurred "many years ago," they understand it was further in the past than something that happened yesterday. Older preschoolers make use of visual cues, such as the style of dress or the type of technology, to judge whether images are from a long time in the past or closer to the present (Jantz & Seefeldt, 1999).

Preschoolers also develop a growing sense of time by understanding and using words related to sequence. Terms such as *before* and *after*, *first* and *last*, *then* and *next*, give them a way to grasp and talk about the passage of time. So history for young children, rather than being about specific periods, is more about the sequence of events, and how much "earlier" or "later" things occur.

These developments show preschoolers can engage with history if it is related to the sequence — the story — of their own lives (Egan, 1989). Just as talking about what already happened in a storybook allows children to anticipate what might happen next, they can begin to contemplate future events in their own lives ("Last night we bought tomato plants. When I get home from school today, I'm going to help plant them"). A growing awareness of yesterday, today, and tomorrow is the groundwork upon which preschoolers build a sense of their own roles in society.

# Teaching Strategies That Support History

Preschool children show a growing awareness of time and are increasingly able to sequence events. These developments give them the foundation to appreciate history, especially when they can connect it to personal narratives. To help young children use these capabilities as they engage with history in meaningful ways, adults can employ the teaching strategies described here.

## Support children's awareness of present, recent past, and short-term future events

The HighScope daily routine provides an ideal structure to help children organize ideas about time. Use the schedule to call attention to current, recent, and upcoming events. Use pictures, photos, cards, and representative objects to help children visualize and sequence the parts of the day. Refer to the order of activities — what just happened, what will happen next.

You can also take photos to track specific activities, such as a work-time construction project or field trip. Provide puzzles that are solved in sequence (such as nesting dolls or stacking donuts) and photograph or trace pictures of each step. Order the pictures with the children, and talk about children's use of words such as *before* and *after, first* and *last, next* and *then,* and *earlier* and *later.*

**Planning and recall times.** Planning and recall in particular provide daily opportunities for children to anticipate and review their activities, and to do so in sequence as their cognitive capacities expand. The plan-do-review process often mimics the "cyclical" pattern of history. As children share what they did at work time, they may plan to continue or expand the activity the next day. In this way, the past becomes the basis for the future. Work-in-progress signs carry this same message: "I enjoyed working with these materials (or friends) today, and I want to continue working with them tomorrow."

*At the end of small-group time, Darya describes her collage to the teacher. "I taped red felt in this corner, then I glued and sprinkled sequins all over. I'm not done with this part, though. I need more lace." She puts her collage on a shelf and puts a work-in-progress sign beside it. "I'm going to glue the lace tomorrow at work time. Maybe I will add more sequins when I finish."*

**Message board.** The message board is another concrete way to remind children of the recent past and near future. For example, if you introduced a new material at small-group time yesterday, you can indicate on the message board where children will find it today if they

*This child uses wooden figures to indicate where she will play during work time — the period that immediately follows planning time.*

choose to play with it. If an important event (such as field trip) is coming up, you can use concrete objects or symbols to count down the days. If the weekend is ahead, you can write two symbols (for example, a schoolhouse with an "X" through it) to indicate that the next two days are "no school" days. Some teachers make a circular calendar representing a week, with five of the same symbol to indicate school days and two of a different symbol for the stay-at-home days. Children then have a visual of time as a continuum or cycle.

*Looking at the drawing of the computer on the message board, Franklin says excitedly, "That's the fruit game we played yesterday! Timmy, wanna play with me today?"*

*At arrival time on a Friday, Simone sees a picture of two school buildings surrounded by red circles and X's through them. "No school tomorrow," she says. "Then we go to church. Then school again."*

**Group times.** Another way to establish a foundation for understanding time and history is to play sequencing games at group times. For example, plan a large-group activity doing two movements in order (first tap your ears and then tap your shoulders). Give children the opportunity to be leaders and to tell, as well as show, the movement sequence to their classmates. Do the same thing with music activities (sing two notes that vary in pitch or loudness). As children become adept at these movement and music activities, increase them to sequences of three or more motions or notes.

**Special events.** Celebrate holidays and other special occasions if and only if they are meaningful to children at that time. Events that are significant on the grown-up calendar may only be relevant to children if their families

are preparing for, commemorating, or following up the occasion. For events that do matter, keep in mind that just because they are over for adults does not mean children are ready to let go of them. Halloween pretend play may linger through Thanksgiving; a birthday party may remain important for weeks, and even reemerge on the occasion of another child's celebration. Likewise, future events (an upcoming road trip to visit grandma and grandpa) may assume substantial significance in a child's mind. Anticipatory pretend play as well as follow-up reenactments may occur for a long time. When children themselves choose to observe these special events, they provide teachers with many opportunities to scaffold their sense of history, along with an awareness of diversity, geography, and other domains of social studies.

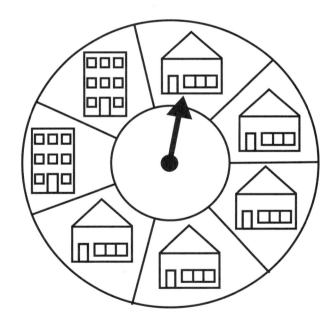

*In this urban setting, the low building with the peaked roof, door, and long horizontal window represents the preschool. The tall building with three floors of windows and a door represents the apartment houses where most children live. Five "school" symbols represent the five days of school. Two "apartment" symbols represent the two days children stay home. The arrow is turned to indicate each day, returning to the starting point as each new week begins.*

### Use concrete representations to make children aware of the distant past and far future

Just as books, artwork, music, and other concrete representations acquaint children with different places in geography, so too can these resources expand their awareness of more distant past and future times. Young children are interested in learning about how people used to dress, cook, travel, build houses, and so on. Likewise, through media exposure, they can imagine "futuristic" settings where people have superpowers, travel in unusual vehicles, and use fantastic equipment to accomplish their goals.

Since they are constantly discovering new realities in today's world, young children are just as ready to accept what the past was like as what may occur in the far future. At the same time, they understand that these depictions do not represent the present. That is, they can connect these other periods to their own lives while still knowing if they are historical or set in the future. For example, if they've gone camping and made dinner over an open fire, it may not seem far-fetched to them that people once cooked all their meals that way. Likewise, if they've seen photos of astronauts walking on the moon, they might imagine that someday people will wear spacesuits all the time.

To support children's interest in time periods other than their own, read books (e.g., Tomie de Paola's *Mother Goose*) and sing songs (e.g., "Oh Susannah") that are clearly set in different times. Bring in artwork depicting other eras. Talk about historical characters and how their lives matched or differed from how people live today ("Simple Simon wore short pants called knickers but he liked pies same as you"; "Susannah traveled

*Reading books set in different time periods helps children understand how people have lived in different eras.*

in a covered wagon instead of a car"). Do the same with stories set in the future that feature spaceships, robots, or odd-looking houses and vehicles.

Further, as you talk with children about their representations and join as a partner in their play, use and encourage them to use an expanding vocabulary of time and sequence words. Begin with terms such as *before* and *after, first* and *last, yesterday* and *tomorrow.* Then introduce expressions such *once upon a time, then* and *now, a long time ago,* and *when I grow up.* As noted throughout this book, language affects thought. Therefore, hearing and using these time-related sequencing words will help children think about the passage of time within the broader sweep of history.

*At work time in the art area, while making what he calls a "work" out of Lego blocks, Joey says, "When I grow up I'm gonna ride a motorcycle*

*and take Jake (his younger brother) to school. That's my job. I'm gonna have kids. Jake is mine because I won't go to school because I'm a big boy."*

*At snacktime, Bryan tells the group, "When we went to the powwow, I danced the bear dance with Grandpa John. That's how they did it in the old days, before I was born. He's a chief."*

For examples of how children demonstrate their growing understanding of history, and how you can support their learning at different stages of development, see "Ideas for Scaffolding KDI 57. History." The suggestions in the chart, together with those described above, will help you support and gently extend preschoolers' emerging ideas about history as you play and interact with them.

# Ideas for Scaffolding KDI 57. History

Always support children at their current level and occasionally offer a gentle extension.

| Earlier | Middle | Later |
|---|---|---|
| *Children may* | *Children may* | *Children may* |
| • Refer to past and future events without saying how far in the past or future they occur (e.g., six months ahead, say, "Pretty soon it's my birthday"; say, of their toddler brother, "Yesterday I got a brother"). | • Describe or represent events from earlier that day or the day before, or happening later that day or the next day (e.g., at pickup time, tell a parent, "I made you a picture at work time"; at snacktime, say, "My aunt is picking me up, and I'm sleeping at her house tonight"). | • Describe or represent events from several days or more in the past, or happening several days or more in the future (e.g., at work time, when reading a book about grandparents, say, "My nana came to visit a long time ago at Thanksgiving"). |
| • Wait for the teacher to announce the next activity in the daily routine (not anticipate events in a sequence) or anticipate the next immediate event in a familiar sequence (e.g., at the end of large-group time, go to the coat rack because they know outside time comes next). | • Describe a sequence of two events that happened (past) or that will happen (future) (e.g., upon arriving at school, Leah announces, "We watched a bird at the feeder, then we came to school"; at large-group time, Caitlin says, "Next we play outside, then we go home!"). | • Describe a sequence of three or more events that happened (past) or that will happen (future) (e.g. "Jason and I picked pumpkins and ate apples and came back and carved jack-o-lanterns"; make a plan to paint a picture, dress up, and then play on the computer "if there's time"). |
| *To support children's current level, adults can* | *To support children's current level, adults can* | *To support children's current level, adults can* |
| • Take the lead from children; talk about their present interests and concerns (e.g., "Tell me about what you did with the blocks"; "You're excited about your birthday"). | • Talk about events that happened or will happen within a 24-hour period (e.g., "You rode the bus this morning with your mommy"; "We have to wait until snacktime to eat the cupcakes"). | • Share experiences that happened in the same time frame the children refer to (e.g., "My sister came to visit me a long time ago at Thanksgiving too"). |
| • Use sequencing words such as *first, next, last, then, before,* and *after* (e.g., "You got your coat because you knew that outside time was next"). | • Ask children to remember or predict more than one step in a sequence (e.g., "What did you do after mixing the paint and getting a brush?"; "I wonder what things you'll do after planting the peas"). | • Provide opportunities for children to represent a sequence of actions or events (e.g., to draw or show during recall time what they did at work time; make up songs and stories; take dictation about multistep events). |
| *To offer a gentle extension, adults can* | *To offer a gentle extension, adults can* | *To offer a gentle extension, adults can* |
| • Add a concrete time frame to children's statements (e.g., "It will be your birthday after lots of days of school"; "You got a brother back at Christmas"). | • Model the use of time words such as *yesterday, today, tomorrow, earlier,* and *later* (e.g., "You played with the wooden blocks yesterday"; "Tomorrow is our field trip"). | • Encourage children to elaborate their descriptions of past and future events (e.g., "It was summer and very hot when your nana visited. Tell me what you did while she was here"). |
| • Call children's attention to the daily routine chart; encourage them to point to or move the clothespin to the next part of the daily routine (e.g., Point and say, "Recall time is after cleanup time"). | • Help children recall multistep sequences (e.g., take photos of building projects or field trips they can arrange in order). | • Encourage children to give multistep, sequenced instructions (e.g., at work time, ask what order to do the tasks they assign you to get ready for a party). |

# CHAPTER 8

# KDI 58. Ecology

## H. Social Studies

## 58. Ecology: Children understand the importance of taking care of their environment.

· · · · · · · · · · · · · · · · · · · · · · · · · · · · · · · · · · · · · · · · · · · · · ·

**Description:** Children share responsibility for taking care of their environment inside and outside the classroom (e.g., picking up litter, watering plants, sorting things into recycling bins). They understand that their actions affect the well-being of the environment.

*At planning time, Petra makes a plan to water the plants in the house area. "But not the cactus," she says. "They're from the desert and if they get too much water, they die!"*

*At the end of small-group time, Chris puts the bent paper clips in the recycling bin for metal and the torn magazines into the recycling bin for paper.*

*After signaling cleanup time, Garrison turns the light switch to the "off" position. When his teacher asks why he did this, Garrison responds, "I'm leaving them off to save energy. My dad is always yelling at us to 'Turn off the lights!'"*

*At arrival, Leona shakes her head and clucks her tongue. "Those bad guys," she tsks, "they dumped wrappers and butts in the parking lot. They're making the planet all dirty!"*

In the HighScope Curriculum, ecology is listed under social studies rather than science. Of course, learning about the natural world, including the environment, is part of science education too (KDI 51. Natural and physical world). However, ecology is more broadly concerned with people taking responsibility for that environment. It involves understanding the interdependence between humans and nature, and how people can and should act as caretakers of the planet. Because this relationship entails social actions, ecology fits within social studies. This approach is also consistent with the curriculum developed by the World Forum Nature Action Collaborative for Children (2010, para. 1), which states in its universal principles for children:

"We believe that regular connections with the natural world encourage children to develop:

- Respect for local cultures and climates and for themselves as part of nature.

- Feelings of unity, peace and well-being as global citizens."

Young children learn to see ecology as being relevant to themselves by considering how their actions and those of others affect the well-being of their immediate environment. Given their emerging interest in other times and places (history and geography), they are also able to think about the world beyond their door and what might happen to the environment in the future.

# Influences on Children's Ideas About Ecology

An emerging body of research shows the harmful effects of children's disconnection from nature, and the benefits of strengthening those ties. On the downside is the fact that young children's fears and misconceptions about nature are growing (Sobel, 1996). For example, images of natural disasters may make them afraid of ordinary wind and rain; if their main experience with animals is pets, children have little idea of how animals live in the wild, seek food, or use their sense of smell or hearing to get around in the dark.

The prevalence of screen time in today's society also means children play outdoors much less than in previous generations (American Academy of Pediatrics, 2001). Not only can this lead to deleterious health effects, but children acquire their ideas about nature through the media instead of direct contact with living things (Cohen & Horm-Wingerd, 1993). The images they receive are often negative, causing them to become anxious or even develop "biophobia" — a fear of the natural world and ecological problems (White & Stoecklin, 2008). For example, interviews with children from preschool to age nine found that their attitudes toward the natural environment (plants, animals, weather) included more expressions of fear and dislike than of appreciation, caring, or enjoyment (Simmons, 1994). Moreover, immersion in the media means children are bombarded with messages that say material goods are essential to self-fulfillment. "Research shows that children with more materialistic values are less likely to engage in environmentally sustainable behavior such as recycling or conserving water" (Linn, 2010, p. 65).

By contrast, there is mounting evidence that for young children "repeated, regular, and sustained positive experiences in the natural environment are influential for attaining sustainable behaviors and lifestyles" (Samuelsson & Kaga, 2010, p. 58). Children who play outside care more about the environment that offers them opportunities to explore, build, and move. Efforts to limit exposure to commercialism and connect children with nature also reveal that children play more creatively in green space (Linn, 2010). Exposure to nature appears to promote early development in other areas as well, including health and physical fitness (Fjortoft, 2001), language arts (Miller, 2007), sustained attention (Taylor, Kuo, & Sullivan, 2001), collaborative social relationships (Moore, 1996), and overall emotional well-being and mental health (Wells & Evans, 2003).

# Developmental Understanding of Ecological Concepts

Children's ideas about ecology develop primarily in conjunction with their emerging social skills, particularly empathy and a sense of community. Their developing understanding of basic scientific principles about the natural world further helps them apply these social abilities specifically to taking care of the environment.

**Social-emotional learning and ecology.** Children's emotions, attitudes, and values about nature develop earlier than their abstract, logical, and rational perspectives (Kellert, 2002). They need to develop "biophilia" — a love for nature — before they can learn about the Earth academically and become its guardians (Sobel, 2008). The problem with most environmental education programs is that they teach children abstract concepts first, including many that are beyond their understanding, and feature global problems that are beyond their control. Instead of producing concern, such programs result in fear and feelings of powerlessness. That is why teaching nature abstractly in the classroom does not lead to pro-environmental behaviors later in life (Schultz, 2000).

Based on these developmental social considerations, "during early childhood, the main objective of environmental education should be the development of empathy between the child and the natural world" (White & Stoecklin, 2008, para. 11). This includes regular opportunities to play in nature, take care of plants, and cultivate relationships with animals — both real and imaginary (Sobel, 1996). The emergence of empathy in preschoolers (KDI 10. Empathy) makes them capable of showing concern for other people and for wildlife. In addition, children this age are becoming members of the community. They can take responsibility for its physical care, such as picking up litter, feeding pets, or planting a garden. While their primary affiliation is to their own communities of home and school, explorations in geography (KDI 56. Geography) mean preschoolers have an emerging understanding of wider-reaching communities. Thus they are able to show concern about animal and plant life in environments they may not have encountered themselves.

**Science learning and ecology.** In terms of scientific development, preschoolers are learning about the natural and physical world (KDI 51. Natural and physical world). They can identify what living things need to survive and thrive (food, water, shelter, and warmth). They also have a preliminary understanding of

*Observing and learning about plants and animals helps children develop empathy with the natural world.*

basic scientific processes, such as how energy transforms things (heat melts ice; flowing water moves things in its path). Moreover, preschoolers use resources to accomplish their personal goals (paper to draw on, clay to build with). They therefore have an emerging awareness that certain resources may be in limited supply and may run out in the future. This recognition is tied to their learning about history, and being able to imagine not only the past but also future time (KDI 59. History). Participating in concrete activities such as recycling and conserving light and water therefore makes sense to them.

## Teaching Strategies That Support Ecology

Research shows that informal experiences are "more effective than direct teaching or preaching in helping young children internalize values and develop desirable attitudes and leanings" toward the environment and ecology (Samuelsson & Kaga, 2010, p. 60). Based on these findings, early childhood professionals from 16 countries met in Gothenburg, Sweden in 2007 and 2008, and recommended that early childhood education focus on "7Rs" (examples added by author):

- *Reduce* involves working with parents and educators to find ways to mediate children's exposure to advertisements promoting endless consumption. For example, adults can help children learn the difference between what they want and what they need.

- *Reuse* involves showing children how materials can be used many times for different purposes in preschool and at home. For example, adults can comment that the scrap paper children are drawing on the back of was once a letter. They can take children to a nearby park whose running track is made from ground-up tires.

- *Recycle* means asking children to recycle materials at school and to bring recyclables to school that can be integrated into a wide range of activities. For example, children enjoy separating and sorting materials into recycling bins. They know that many of the materials they use at school come from home (empty food containers in the house area; golf tees in the woodworking area; and old magazines and catalogs in the book area).

- *Respect* involves nurturing an understanding of and regard for nature and natural processes, and minimizing the extent to which they are violated. For example, children can learn to gather fallen leaves, bark, and branches rather than stripping them from trees. They can learn to handle classroom pets gently and look after their needs for food, water, and a clean place to sleep.

- *Reflect* means thinking about the impact of our actions on nature. For example, children can see how flowers and vegetables thrive when people water and weed the school garden, or conversely, what happens when they forget to take care of it.

- *Repair* involves taking care of broken toys and other objects and repairing them rather than discarding them. For example, children can bring broken objects to adults to be fixed. They can help to repair nondangerous objects, such as taping the ripped cover of a book. Children can also learn how to prevent the need for unnecessary repairs by taking good care of things to begin with.

- *Responsibility* is about recognizing when children accomplish something they are proud of, which puts them on an equal footing with adults. For example, when adults acknowledge children for cleaning up a spill or caring for a pet, they show they value children's abilities.

Because young children are keen observers of nature and are socially motivated to be helpful members of their community, they are ready to engage with many environmental concerns. To incorporate the ideas addressed by the 7Rs in an active-learning setting, you can use the strategies described here to make ecology a concrete, relevant, and meaningful subject for preschoolers.

## Develop children's awareness of and appreciation for nature

As noted previously, the first step in making children care about the environment is fostering a personal connection with nature. The more young children enjoy the sensations of the natural world, and develop empathy for living things, the more meaningful their concerns about ecology will become as they get older. Make nature a concrete reality, not an abstraction.

Help parents understand why it is important for their children to engage in less "screen time" and more "outdoor time." Although not all families will resonate to statements on behalf of ecology, they can appreciate nature's benefits to their children's physical and mental health, creativity, and intellectual development. If safety concerns are an issue in the neighborhood, you can facilitate parent advocacy groups

*Children need to spend time outdoors each day, to develop a positive, personal connection to nature.*

to encourage civic leaders to establish safe play zones, or help parents network with one another to construct play yards on nonschool grounds.

Except for extreme weather conditions, include time in your daily routine for children to go outside every day — once for a half-day program and twice for a full-day program. Encourage children to feel the sun and wind on their faces. Talk about how the air feels when it is hot or cold; sunny, drizzling, or snowing. Examine the plants native to your area, and observe how they change with the seasons. Plant a garden. Look at the birds, insects, and animals that thrive in your area. Talk about where and how they live, and whether they disappear and return at certain times of the year. Make and install bird feeders. Feel different types of soil (sand and clay, smooth and pebbly dirt) and talk about which ones are good for building things or growing flowers and vegetables. Walk around the neighborhood and go on field trips to experience different local environments (for example, farms, forests, beaches, lakes, streams, or urban gardens).

In short, help children simultaneously develop what might seem like contradictory attitudes: (1) The outdoors is something "ordinary" to be experienced every day; and (2) Nature is something "extraordinary" that evokes a sense of wonder. These coexisting attitudes can instill appreciation for the natural environment. Then, as children become increasingly capable of understanding threats to the environment, they will have the emotional commitment needed to take action.

## Provide opportunities for children to take care of the indoor classroom and outdoor learning environment

When children play a meaningful role in taking care of the learning environment, it supports the development of empathy and sense of community that are at the heart of children's emerging ecological awareness. Appropriate activities and opportunities for preschoolers include

- Taking care of materials and using them properly to avoid breakage and other damage (e.g., putting tops on markers so they do not dry out, handling dress-up clothes carefully so they do not tear, not banging or throwing mechanical tools or electronics)

- Cleaning up (putting away) materials in their designated places so others can find them

- Helping with simple repairs (gluing a wooden letter back on an area sign; taping the torn corner of the snack chart)

- Taking care of pets (changing the water in their bowls, feeding them, shredding paper for their cages)

- Picking up litter in the hallway and on the playground (under adult supervision and with appropriate safety measures to avoid broken glass, contamination, or other dangers)

Comment on how children's actions help to maintain the school environment for everyone's use. Acknowledge when they are being careful handling materials. Encourage their efforts rather than praising them for being "good helpers."

*At work time, Franklin puts fresh water in Tippy's (the guinea pig's) bowl and watches him lap it up. "Sometimes I'm so thirsty I can lap a whole bowl of water too!" Franklin comments.*

*At work time in the house area, Lyle uses cloth towels to wipe up the water he spills "making spaghetti." His teacher says, "Lyle, you wiped up every drop of water on the floor. Now we don't have to worry about someone slipping and getting hurt."*

Moreover, familiarity with the outdoors allows them to develop positive rather than fearful attitudes about nature.

*Arriving a bit late to school, Gabriella announces, "We had to stop the car 'cause deer were crossing the road! We waited and waited. There was so many of them!" Her teacher asks if Gabriella and her mother counted the deer. "I counted the two babies," replies Gabriella. "Their mommy walked behind them to make sure they were safe."*

*At outside time, Aaron picks up several pieces of newspaper that have blown under the climber. He tells his teacher, "Me and Timmy [his brother] and dad helped clean up the road [highway]. We wore orange stripy things [vests] and gloves. I got to carry a big trash bag."*

*At large-group time, Camille plants lettuce seeds in the class vegetable garden. She tells her teacher, "When they grow, everybody can have lettuce salad for lunch."*

## Connect children's personal environments to the world environment

Many of the children's actions, such as reusing and recycling materials, can be connected to the world beyond the preschool. As preschoolers' sense of the environment expands beyond their immediate community, comment on how their actions contribute to the well-being of the planet. Remember to focus on children's positive actions, without worrying or frightening them about environmental problems they are too young to understand or have control over.

*During cleanup time, children learn to take good care of the classroom environment.*

❖

*At cleanup time, Jennifer says, "Wow! There's lots of blocks to put away. I need help!" Abby and Brad immediately offer to assist her. When all the blocks are shelved, their teacher says, "You did it! Now the floor is all clear for large-group time."*

Be sure children have opportunities to take responsibility outdoors as well as indoors. Just as you do at work time, give children a warning so they know that soon they will have to start cleaning up the loose toys and return them and the wheeled vehicles to storage. As already noted, playing outside also helps develop children's empathy for plant and animal life.

*This child learns about the desert environment during a class field trip to a botanical garden greenhouse.*

*On a field trip to a papermaking plant, the children watched wood pulp being converted into paper. They also saw how scrap paper was re-pulped. At small-group time the next day, as Rollo put paper scraps in the recycling bin, he said, "Now we don't have to cut down a tree."*

*At message board, the teacher draws a leaky faucet with an X through it and asks if anyone knows what it means. Cindy runs to the sink and announces, "It's not dripping anymore." The teacher explains that the plumber fixed it yesterday and says, "Now we won't waste any more water." Todd comments, "My mommy changed the wisher (washer) on our sink too. She said a drop every day wastes a gazillion gallons. That's a lot of water!"*

Take advantage of naturally occurring situations to help children connect their own lives and familiar settings to other people and situations on the planet. For example, the leaky sink incident led to a discussion about wasting water on a gigantic scale. As your center switches from incandescent bulbs to compact fluorescent lamps (CFLs), you can talk about conserving electricity. Children may have heard parents talk about turning off lights when they leave a room, or shutting off electronics not in use. Encourage them to share the steps they and their families are taking at home, and talk about how people living in many different places are equally concerned and are enacting similar measures.

Sometimes environmental disasters, which can arouse anxiety in the families who are directly affected by them, provide opportunities for learning. Pretend play and sympathetic conversations can also help children regain a sense of control during stressful times. Describing how teachers and preschoolers on the Gulf Coast dealt with the 2010 British Petroleum Company oil spill, HighScope field consultant Tricia Kruse (2010) offered the following examples:

- At greeting time, one child announced, "There's oil on our beaches." The children shared their experiences going to the beach with their families. They talked about swimming, building sand castles, and fishing, and how they could no longer enjoy those activities. Their teacher reassured them that cleanup was underway (the children understood the idea of "cleanup") and that everyone hoped to someday resume the activities they enjoyed.

- The children mixed cooking oil and water at small-group time. They observed how the oil floated on the surface no matter how much they stirred the mixture. Instead of focusing on the negative, this activity channeled their curiosity and sense of wonder.

- A child whose mother volunteered to clean wildlife pretended to buy and use dish soap to clean toy animals at work time. This role playing made the child feel helpful, like an adult.

- At work time, children pretended to "interview" one another on television and made comments into the "microphone" (a small block) such as "I feel bad for the animals" and "My Uncle Rick is helping on Pensacola Beach." Again, children expressed their concerns in a safe setting and felt good that adults they knew were providing meaningful help.

- Children drew pictures about their experiences at work time and small-group time. One child captioned hers, "Shells, crabs, and water covered in oil." Representing their experiences encouraged children to think about what was happening in greater detail.

- Children and parents brought in newspaper photos and made a book for the class library. This was a concrete activity that allowed children to reflect on their experiences. Since many of the photos were of images they had not directly experienced, the book also helped to broaden their perspective of the people and wildlife affected by the oil spill.

- Parents shared with the teachers what their children said at home. One boy told his mom, "I don't know what is wrong with this world, but I haven't been swimming in a long time!" Expressing feelings in a supportive environment helped children cope with them in positive ways. Adults were able to validate these emotions without either provoking further anxiety or offering false promises. They could simply say they felt the same way the children did.

For examples of how children demonstrate their awareness of nature and concern for the environment, and how adults can support and gently extend their learning at different developmental levels, see "Ideas for Scaffolding KDI 58. Ecology." Use the above strategies, and additional ideas presented in the chart, to scaffold preschoolers' emerging understanding of ecology during your daily play and other interactions with them.

# Ideas for Scaffolding KDI 58. Ecology

Always support children at their current level and occasionally offer a gentle extension.

| Earlier | Middle | Later |
|---|---|---|

*Children may*

- Care for the indoor or outdoor environment when asked or reminded to (e.g., they may throw their tissue on the ground unless reminded; they may recycle materials when a peer says, "You have to put the paper there [in the paper bin], not in the garbage").

*Children may*

- Take care of things in the environment that they are personally interested in (e.g., water the flower they planted; move a ladybug from the wagon to a safer place).

*Children may*

- Take responsibility for the care of things in the environment; recognize their actions have an effect on the environment (e.g., "Sniffy has no water. Can you help me get the bottle out of his cage so I can fill it?"; "We could save these yogurt cups to put paint in"; remind others to recycle their paper scraps).

*To support children's current level, adults can*

- Remind children to help take care of the environment themselves (e.g., remind them to throw tissues in the trash; point out the recycling bins and what goes in each) rather than criticizing them when they don't; model for children doing it themselves.

*To support children's current level, adults can*

- Acknowledge when children participate in helpful environmental actions (e.g., "You put all the tops on the markers. That's taking care of the materials in our classroom"; "You helped care for the ladybug by moving her to a safer place").

*To support children's current level, adults can*

- Comment on how children's behaviors help the environment (e.g., "Storing the books on the shelf will help keep the pages from tearing"; "Watering the garden helps our vegetables grow").

*To offer a gentle extension, adults can*

- Encourage children to take care of personally meaningful objects and spaces in their environment (e.g., to clean up their toys, put things away in their cubbies, hold the guinea pig gently against their body).

*To offer a gentle extension, adults can*

- Model and describe other ways of taking care of the environment by recycling (e.g., "I'm going to throw the paper in the recycling bin instead of the trash") and reusing (e.g., "Let's save this paper. We can write on the back of it").

*To offer a gentle extension, adults can*

- Solicit children's ideas on ways to reuse and recycle materials (e.g., "If we saved these boxes, what could we do with them?"); encourage children to reflect on how their actions help the environment (e.g., "Why do you think it's good to plant a vegetable garden?").

## Social Studies: A Summary

### General teaching strategies that support social studies

- Build on concrete experiences to help children construct general principles for social understanding and behavior.

- Help children recognize that their personal actions can have a positive effect on the world.

### Teaching strategies that support diversity

- Model respect for diversity.

- Focus on similarities and differences without judgmental comparisons.

- Include diversity in every classroom area and activity.

### Teaching strategies that support community roles

- Provide opportunities for children to learn about and act out different community roles.

- Provide opportunities for children to learn about and act out relationships that involve exchanging money for goods and services.

### Teaching strategies that support decision making

- Provide opportunities for children to solve problems and make plans as a group.

- Encourage children to consider how their choices and decisions affect others.

### Teaching strategies that support geography

- Acquaint children with familiar locations in their community.

- Use concrete representations to connect children to places beyond their own experience.

### Teaching strategies that support history

- Support children's awareness of present, recent past, and short-term future events.

- Use concrete representations to make children aware of the distant past and far future.

### Teaching strategies that support ecology

- Develop children's awareness of and appreciation for nature.

- Provide opportunities for children to take care of the indoor classroom and outdoor learning environment.

- Connect children's personal environments to the world environment.

# References

Aboud, F. E. (2003). The formation of in-group favoritism and out-group prejudice in young children: Are they distinct attitudes? *Developmental Psychology, 39*(1), 48–60. doi:10.1037//0012-1649.39.1.48

Aboud, F. E. (2005). The development of prejudice in childhood and adolescents. In J. F. Dovidio, P. Glick, & L. A. Rudman (Eds.), *On the nature of prejudice: Fifty years after Allport* (pp. 310–326). Malden, MA: Blackwell.

American Academy of Pediatrics, Committee on Public Education. (2001). *Children, adolescents, and television. Pediatrics, 107*(2), 423–426. doi:10.1542/peds.107.2.423

*American Heritage dictionary of the English language* (4th ed.). (2000). Boston, MA: Houghton Mifflin.

Banks, J. (1993). Multicultural education for young children: Racial and ethnic attitudes and their modification. In B. Spodek (Ed.), *Handbook of research on the education of young children* (pp. 236–250). New York, NY: Macmillan.

Barry-Davis, J. (1999). Intuitive understanding of time and space at the age of four. *Dissertation Abstracts International: Section A. Humanities and Social Sciences, 60*(6), 1898.

Barton, K. (1997). History — It can be elementary: An overview of elementary students' understanding of history. *Social Education, 61,* 13–16.

Barton, K., & Levstik, L. (1996). "Back when God was around and everything": Elementary children's understanding of historical time. *American Education Research Journal, 33,* 419–454.

Blades, M. (1998). A cross-cultural study of young children's mapping abilities. *Transactions of the Institute of British Geographers, 23*(2), 269–277.

Carlsson-Paige, N. (2008). *Taking back childhood: Helping your kids thrive in a fast-paced, media-saturated, violence-filled world.* New York, NY: Penguin.

Cohen, S., & Horm-Wingerd, D. (1993). Children and the environment: Ecological awareness among preschool children. *Environment and Behavior, 25*(1), 103–120. doi:10.1177/0013916593251005

Copple, C., & Bredekamp, S. (Eds.). (2009). *Developmentally appropriate practice in early childhood programs serving children from birth through age 8* (3rd ed.). Washington, DC: National Association for the Education of Young Children.

Derman-Sparks, L. (1989). *Anti-bias curriculum: Tools for empowering young children.* Washington, DC: National Association for the Education of Young Children.

Derman-Sparks, L., & Edwards, J. O. (2010). *Anti-bias education for young children and ourselves.* Washington, DC: National Association for the Education of Young Children.

DeVries, R. & Zan, B. (2003). When children make rules. *Educational Leadership, 61*(1), 64–67.

Egan, K. (1989). Layers of historical understanding. *Theory and Research in Social Education, 17,* 280–294.

Egan, K. (1997). The arts as the basics of education. *Childhood Education, 73,* 346–349.

Elias, M. J., Zins, J. E., Weissberg, K. S., Frey, M. T., Greenberg, N. M., Kessler, R., Shriver, T. P. (1997). *Promoting social and emotional learning: Guidelines for educators.* Alexandria, VA: Association for Supervision and Curriculum Development.

Epstein, A. S. (2009). *Me, you, us: Social-emotional learning in preschool.* Ypsilanti, MI: HighScope Press.

Epstein, A. S. (2012). *Social and emotional development.* Ypsilanti, MI: HighScope Press.

Fjortoft, I. (2001). The natural environment as a playground for children: The impact of outdoor play activities in pre-primary school children. *Early Childhood Education Journal, 29*(2), 111–117.

Gartrell, D. (2006). The beauty of class meetings. *Young Children, 61*(6), 54–55.

Geography Education Standards Project (GESP). (1994). *Geography for life: National education standards–1994.* Washington, DC: Author.

Gonzalez-Mena, J. (2007). *Diversity in early care and education: Honoring differences* (5th ed.). New York, NY: McGraw-Hill and Washington, DC: National Association for the Education of Young Children.

Gonzalez-Mena, J. (2008). *Foundations in early childhood education: Teaching children in diverse settings* (4th ed.). New York, NY: McGraw-Hill.

Gouteux, S. (2001). Children's use of geometry and landmarks to reorient in an open space. *Cognition, 81*(2), 119–148.

Gronlund, G. (2006). *Making early learning standards come alive.* St. Paul, MN: Redleaf Press and Washington, DC: National Association for the Education of Young Children.

Harter, S. (1999). *The construction of the self: A developmental perspective.* New York, NY: Guilford.

Harter, S. (2006). The self. In W. Damon, R. M. Lerner, & N. Eisenberg (Eds.), *Handbook of child psychology* (6th ed.): *Social, emotional, and personality development* (Vol. 3, pp. 505–570). New York, NY: Wiley.

Huffman, A. B. (1996). Beyond the weather chart: Weathering new experiences. *Young Children, 51*(5), 34–38.

Jantz, R. K. (1976). Social studies in early childhood education. In C. Seefeldt (Ed.). *Curriculum for the preschool-primary child: A review of the research* (pp. 82–123). Columbus, OH: Merrill.

Jantz, R. K., & Seefeldt, C. (1999). Early childhood social studies. In C. Seefeldt (Ed.), *The early childhood curriculum: Current findings in theory and practice* (3rd ed., pp. 159–178). New York, NY: Teachers College Press.

Kagan, S. L., Britto, P. R., Kauerz, K., & Tarrant, K. (2005). *Early learning and development benchmarks: A guide to young children's learning and development from birth to kindergarten entry.* Olympia, WA: Washington State Department of Early Learning. Retrieved from http://www.del.wa.gov/publications/development/docs/BenchmarksColor.pdf

Kellert, S. R. (2002). *Children and nature: Psychological, sociocultural, and evolutionary investigations.* Cambridge, MA: MIT Press.

Kruse, T. (2010). Oil and water don't mix: The Gulf Coast oil disaster as a preschool social studies lesson. *Exchange, 32*(5), 12–16.

Levin, D. E. (2003). *Teaching young children in violent times: Building a peaceable classroom* (2nd ed.). Washington, DC: Educators for Social Responsibility and National Association for the Education of Young Children.

Levstik, L. (1986). The relationship between historical response and narrative in the classroom. *Theory and Research in Social Education, 14*, 1–15.

Liben, L. S. & Downs, R. M. (1993). Understanding person-space-map relations: Cartographic and developmental perspectives. *Developmental Psychology, 29*(4), 739–752. doi:10.1037//0012-1649.29.4.739

Liben, L. S., & Yekel, C. A. (1996). Preschoolers' understanding of plan and oblique maps: The role of geometric and representational correspondence. *Child Development, 67*, 780–796.

Linn, S. (2010). Commercialism in children's lives. In *Worldwatch Institute: State of the world 2010: Transforming cultures from consumerism to sustainability* (pp. 62–68). New York, NY: W. W. Norton.

Lucier, R., & S. Gainsley. (2005). Amazing days: Celebrating with children and families. In N. A. Brickman, H. Barton, & J. Burd (Eds.), *Supporting young learners 4: Ideas for child care providers and teachers* (pp. 433–441). Ypsilanti, MI: HighScope Press.*

Mayer, R. H. (1995). Inquiry into place as an introduction to world geography—Starting with ourselves. *Social Studies, 86*, 74–77.

Miller, D. L. (2007). The seeds of learning: Young children develop important skills through their gardening experiences at a Midwestern early education program. *Applied Environmental Education and Communication, 6*(2), 49–66.

Mindes, G. (2005). Social studies in today's early childhood curricula. *Young Children, 60*(5), 12–18.

Mitchell, L. S. (1934). *Young geographers.* New York, NY: Bank Street College.

Moore, R. (1996). Compact nature: The role of playing and learning gardens on children's lives. *Journal of Therapeutic Horticulture, 8*, 72–82.

National Association for the Education of Young Children. (2005). *Early childhood program standards and accreditation performance criteria.* Washington, DC: Author.

National Council for the Social Studies. (2010). *National curriculum standards for social studies: A framework for teaching, learning, and assessment.* Silver Spring, MD: Author.

*Also available at the HighScope *Extensions* archive at highscope.org.

Plester, B. (2002). Young children's ability to use aerial photographs as maps. *Children and the Environment, 22*(1), 29–47.

Povinelli, D. J., Landry, A. M., Theall, L. A., Clark, B. R., & Castille, C. M. (1999). Development of young children's understanding that the recent past is causally bound to the present. *Developmental Psychology, 35*(6), 1426–1439.

Ramsey, P. G. (2006). Early childhood multicultural education. In B. Spodek & O. N. Saracho (Eds.), *Handbook of research on the education of young children* (2nd ed., pp. 279–302). Mahwah, NJ: Lawrence Erlbaum.

Samuelsson, I. P., & Kaga, Y. (2010). Early childhood education to transform cultures for sustainability. In *Worldwatch Institute: State of the world 2010: Transforming cultures from consumerism to sustainability* (pp. 57–61). New York, NY: W. W. Norton.

Schultz, P. W. (2000). Empathizing with nature: The effects of perspective taking on concern for environmental education. *Journal of Social Issues, 56*(3), 391–406.

Seefeldt, C. (1993). History for young children. *Theory and Research in Social Education, 21*, 143–155.

Seefeldt, C., Castle, S., & Falconer, R. (2010). *Social studies for the preschool/primary child* (8th ed.). Englewood Cliffs, NJ: Prentice Hall.

Simmons, D. A. (1994). Urban children's preferences for nature: Lessons from environment education. *Children's Environment Quarterly, 11*(3), 194–203.

Sobel, D. (1996). *Beyond ecophobia: Reclaiming the heart of nature education.* Great Barrington, MA: Orion Society.

Sobel, D. (2008). *Children and nature: Design principles for educators.* Portland, ME: Stenhouse.

Soto, L. D. (1999). The multicultural worlds of childhood in postmodern America. In C. Seefeldt (Ed.), *The early childhood curriculum: Current findings in theory and practice* (pp. 218–242). New York, NY: Teachers College Press.

Stea, D., Kirkman, D. D., Pinon, M. F., Middlebrook, N. N., & Rice, J. L. (2004). Preschoolers use maps to find a hidden object outdoors. *Journal of Environmental Psychology, 24*(3), 341–345. doi:10.1016/j.jenvp.2004.05.003

Taylor, A., Kuo, F., & Sullivan, W. (2001). Coping with ADD: The surprising connection to green play settings. *Environment and Behavior, 33*(1), 54–77. doi:10.1177/00139160121972864

Thompson, R. A. (2006). The development of the person: Social understanding, relationships, conscience, self. In W. Damon, R. M. Lerner, & N. Eisenberg (Eds.), *Handbook of child psychology* (6th ed.). *Social, emotional, and personality development* (Vol. 3, pp. 24–98). New York, NY: Wiley.

Thornton, S., & Vukelich, R. (1988). Effects of children's understanding of time concepts on historical understanding. *Theory and Research in Social Education, 16*, 69–82.

Vasilyeva, M. (2002). Solving spatial tasks with unaligned layouts: The difficulty of dealing with conflicting information. *Journal of Experimental Child Psychology, 83*(4), 291–303. doi:10.1016/S0022-0965(02)00151-0

Vasilyeva, M. (2006). Children's use of geometric information in mapping tasks. *Journal of Experimental Child Psychology, 95*(4), 255–277.

Wells, N. M., & Evans, G. W. (2003). Nearby nature: A buffer of life stress among rural children. *Environment and Behavior, 35*(3), 311–330. doi:10.1177/0013916503035003001

White, R., & Stoecklin, V. L. (2008). Nurturing children's biophilia: Developmentally appropriate environmental education for young children. Retrieved from http://www.whitehutchinson.com/children/articles/nurturing.shtml

World Forum Nature Action Collaborative for Children. (2010). *Connecting the world's children with nature environmental action kit.* Retrieved from http://www.worldforumfoundation.org

Wyner, N., & Farquhar, E. (1991). Cognitive, emotional, and social development: Early childhood social studies. In J. Shaver (Ed.), *Handbook of research on social studies teaching and learning* (pp. 101–146). New York, NY: Macmillan.